ENTON BAR

LAID BARE

Some names and identifying details have been changed to protect the privacy of individuals.

Published by Goldcrest Books International Ltd
www.goldcrestbooks.com
publish@goldcrestbooks.com

ISBN: 978-1-911505-67-9
eISBN: 978-1-911505-68-6

This book is dedicated to all the people who are still struggling with their addiction and the people who have come out of the darkness and are living their lives in recovery. One day you will all see the light and your souls will shine.

Peace be with you all.

A NOTE FROM THE AUTHOR

My purpose in writing this book is to help people to understand addiction and to enable drug and alcohol-dependent individuals, who are still living in their whirlwind of destruction, to see that something *decent* can come out of the depths of depravity.

People with addictions come in different shapes and sizes and from all walks of life and cultures.

You may have heard the story of the business journalist and TV presenter who worked hard to get to the top of his profession, He was living life in the fast lane of 1980s London. He had a five-figure salary, lived in luxurious accommodation, which I could only dream about, and had a loving wife and kids. Sadly, he became addicted to alcohol and ended up losing everything and eventually living on the streets.

Even though this same disease tried to overpower my mind, body and soul, I am here today to tell you my story. I am not embarrassed to have been an alcoholic and a drug user; it's what I did under the influence of drugs and alcohol that makes me ashamed. Sharing those stories with you is going to put me a long way out of my comfort zone - but does anything truly great ever happen in your comfort zone?

PROLOGUE

What can I tell you about my alcoholism and my drug taking?

I can tell you about painfulness, monotony, depression, anger, loneliness and euphoria. I can tell you about the worst hangovers imaginable; the worst comedowns imaginable; eating the dirtiest takeaway food ever known; singing *Rock 'n' Roll Star* in the front room of my flat thinking, no, believing, I could do the best impersonation of Liam Gallagher ever; inane conversations that meant nothing at all; preparing and snorting lines of cocaine while getting ready to go out.

I can tell you about having friends and telling them that what was really going on inside me was dangerous. I can tell you about talking to women and getting rejected while they laughed in my face.

I can tell you that once I took so much cocaine, I thought my head was literally going to explode. I can tell you that, one night, I went on a pre-planned all-day bender. An associate had let me stay with him for the night and I woke up to a disgusting smell of urine overpowering the room and realised that I had pissed ***his*** bed with us in it. This was the first time I had urinated in someone else's bed but soiling my own bed was a frequent occurrence. I'd find myself spread-eagled on my floor/bed/settee, completely soiled. Did I feel ashamed? Not for one second. I got showered, when I could, and carried on drinking. It happened again and again.

Was what I did normal? Not many people would think so. Would it make any difference if I told you that there are many people from all walks of life who potentially have done the same? Probably not, but when it comes to drinking and taking drugs, there is no lower, middle or upper class. I am the same as a GP, barrister, airline pilot or city banker living in the most affluent parts of the UK.

Addiction doesn't discriminate by class. The discrimination comes from the way we are viewed by others. I am not reduced by someone's stare, because I do that to myself.

I was not beautiful or desirable, neither was my body. Nobody looked at me. If they did, they would see the horrible veils of flesh that made me.

I've walked down side streets in towns in the early hours of the morning where the street décor was leftover kebabs, chips or whatever you could describe as takeaway food.

I have driven my car under the influence of drink and drugs and thought I was a better driver for it.

I have slept in empty rooms, shivering and dishevelled, but still managed to drink the previous nights' beer, snort the dregs of cocaine and then go about my day.

I have lived on a diet of strong beer (later Jack Daniels) as a 'hair of the dog' to try and regain 'normality'. When that was achieved, I lived on greasy food, takeaways, crisps and chocolate.

I have sat in the bookies with a cup of hot liquid that didn't have the right to be called coffee, just so that I could shelter in the warm.

I used to shower at the local leisure centre and shave in the public toilet, so that I could wash away the 'hobo' look, if only for a day or two.

When I was street homeless, I remember standing beside my tent in the pitch black and holding down so much sadness that I couldn't sense anything anymore. Sorrow and anger tarnished all my feelings. The only thing I wanted was to drink myself into oblivion.

Sometimes, I reminisced about what felt to me then like the 'good old days' when a regular supply of work meant that money was never a problem; when I felt, for a brief time, that I belonged to the 'in-crowd'. I could spend up to £200 on a designer shirt if I wanted. Now, I see it as a sullied, fantasy life that only brought pain to me and to those around me.

CHAPTER 1

A 1980s childhood

I was born on July 23, 1976, at the Leicester Royal Infirmary. My mum always reminds me that it was 'the heatwave year'. My actual due date was August 13, so I wasted no time in coming into the world!

My parents were living in Sileby, Leicestershire, because my grandad was experiencing some health issues. After a short stay, my grandad's health improved, and my parents moved back with me to our family home in Pembrokeshire.

I was a very sensitive child with a heightened level of anxiety. I was pretty much scared of everything. Sometimes I got so scared that I thought I was going to pee myself, but I knew I couldn't because it would get me into trouble.

The world was too big for me and it took a very long time for me to find the right space in it.

I had a stable upbringing, mainly because my parents gave me consistency and routine. My family was unassuming and close-knit. There was mum, dad, my two younger brothers and me.

My mum was from a big Romany gypsy family and she was one of 11 children. Everyone in the village knew who the

Boswells were and I'm not talking about the family of the same name from the 1980s TV sitcom *Bread!*

My dad was from a smaller family. He was one of four. He was originally from Sileby and he met my mum while he was working in Haverfordwest on a painting contract. Lord knows why he ended up there, but the rest is history.

There's only a three-year gap between us boys. My middle brother Jason was shy and loved animals. My youngest brother Justin was what my mum and dad would call a 'ring-tail', which basically means a mischievous individual. Boy, was he! We grew up in a little village that few have heard of called Johnston, in Pembrokeshire, in a three-bedroom council house.

I was always afraid of something, but I loved playing sport. There was no internet when I was growing up in the 80s and early 90s, and only four TV channels.

Brick-like mobile phones were just coming in, and still a rarity. Apple was something you ate out of a fruit bowl or left on your teacher's desk.

If I needed to get somewhere 30 years ago, my brain sent a message to my legs, which then engaged in the miracle known as walking.

If I wanted to meet my mates down the park, or at the youth club, we all did this weird thing where we agreed to meet at a set time, and then when that time came around, we all turned up. It really was mind-boggling behaviour.

If we couldn't meet for some reason, then the next best thing was to walk to their houses. If their bikes were outside then I knew that my friends would be in.

I never had an Xbox or PlayStation to play on all night. I had an Atari to start with and later, when my mum bought it from the charity shop (her idea of shopping heaven), a Commodore 64, but there was no chance of playing it late into the evening.

Inside the house we had all the warmth we needed. Most nights I would have a bath, as there wasn't a shower until much later. Home-cooked meals were on the table every night except when there was enough money for us to have a 'chippy tea', usually on a Friday night.

My mum would do housework until the cows came home. The house would be cleaned from top to bottom every day. Patches were sewn on my clothes to cover up holes and not as a fashion statement. When my mum got fed up of me 'playing her up' she would utter the words 'Wait till your dad gets back', and that was enough to make me think very carefully about whatever I was doing.

Sundays, though, were very different and probably the best day of the week for me.

Firstly, Sunday was roast dinner day: oven on, chicken in. All the vegetables were prepared in the morning and would be put on to boil at just the right time. The smell got your mouth watering and your stomach would be crying out to you with the rumbling noises it made.

While dinner was cooking, my dad would be down at the local watering hole, supping a few lagers. When he came back, he was the designated carver of the roast chicken. There was no electric carving tool in our house. Instead we had an old-fashioned sharpening rod and I still have fond memories of dad sharpening the knife until it could have taken your hand off.

Sunday night was the one time my brothers and I had to share the bath water and, luckily for me, being the oldest I got to go first. Funnily enough it was the only night where my brothers would leave me to my own devices because they quickly caught on that I would leave them with a 'watery' gift in the bath water if they pissed me off.

Sunday would also be the night that my mum would iron my school uniform and put it over the bannisters ready for me to put on the next morning.

There was always music playing in our house. My dad had a vast music collection: Motown, George Benson, Luther Vandross, Alexander O'Neill and many other bands and solo artists that became part of my musical education. Mum's radio was always playing too. Her favourites were *Our Tune* and *Pick of the Pops. Our Tune* was a sentimental segment originally presented by Simon Bates on his BBC Radio One mid-morning show. It featured a true story sent in by a listener together with a song that they associated with this event. Many of these stories were tearjerkers, although some had happy endings.

Pick of the Pops was presented during my childhood by Alan 'Fluff' Freeman. It counted down the Top 20s from the charts of years gone by. Its theme tune still stays in my head today.

My dad was a painter and decorator by trade, but he was much more than that. He had fingers in many pies. A jack of all trades, always good at whatever he put his hand to, he always had something to do. The only time my dad would be in the house was when the daylight hours ran out.

I watched him build a shed from scratch which, at first, had room for our dog Lucky. Then, when he decided to breed pigeons, he moved Lucky to a purpose-built dog run and kennel at the side of the shed. He bought and installed a wood burner in his shed and put up a dartboard for my brothers and me to play darts in the warm during the winter.

It would seem there was nothing that my dad couldn't make. My mum describes him as a loveable rogue. From what my Grandma told me he had an affinity with the outdoors from an early age and was a 'bush tucker man' long before the likes of Ray Mears and Bear Grylls.

Some of my dad's hobbies were fishing, ferreting and lamping. Ferreting, or hunting with ferrets, is a pastime that has been around since the 12th century. It fulfils the important job of managing rabbit populations in areas where they are an agricultural pest.

Lamping is the same process only using dogs, a greyhound, whippet or lurcher crossbreed, and a lamp at night. I may be biased, but my dad excelled at this. He made his own nets and spent hour after hour nurturing his ferrets and dogs to help him accomplish the end goal.

I loved going ferreting and lamping with him. As much as I was afraid of going out in the dark, and the rabbits he caught, I just loved being with my dad. Watching him in his element was awe-inspiring and because he made me feel safe it became enjoyable. I just hope he knew that these were the times I could connect to him. Unfortunately, I was never going to have the 'bush tucker' trait in me. I loved the outdoors for other reasons.

My mum was born to be a mother. After a few spells of employment in her younger years, my mum met dad and soon started a family and became the housewife.

From an early age, I was always pinned to her side and always quick to get some TLC. She made sure that I knew that I was always valued.

In the 80s and 90s we had to find our own fun. The one place I had the most fun was Cocky's Woods.

Cocky's Woods was such a simple place. It just seemed to pull my friends and me to it like a magnet. Rope swings were made and hung from certain trees and one of them swung you right out over a pond. I always held my breath for fear that I would end up in the water. I did of course, just like many of my friends. Cocky's Pond would always get you in the end!

Fishing occupied me for hours. The pond was big enough for roach and eels to live in. This type of excitement suited me and the many hours that I spent fishing with my friends and family helped me. I didn't feel nervous or anxious then. I was in a safe environment, enjoying the thrills that were coming my way.

Away from Cocky's Wood and around my estate, my friends and I used to go 'hedge chopping'. This involved charging at random hedges in front of anyone's garden and throwing yourself into or over them to make each other laugh. Fast forward 30 years and I think to myself how stupid I must have looked launching myself through the leaves and sticks and landing on my face in someone's front yard!

Scrumping, which is stealing apples from someone's tree, was another popular pastime. There used to be a house on Langford Road which had the best apples in the village and every year my friends and I would scrump there. Delicious!

Jumping on the back of the milkman's float, trying not to get caught when he stopped, was a thrill. Then there was 'knock-knock run'. This 'game' of knocking on someone's door and running away was great fun to start with, but we had to up the ante. Someone suggested that we should wrap some dog poo in newspaper and the new game became setting it on fire just before the front door opened. I remember one time my dad had told me in no uncertain terms that I had to look after my younger brother, much to my displeasure. To get my own back, I made him put the newspaper containing dog poo on to a neighbours' front doorstep and light it.

I didn't know it, but the neighbour had got wise to what was going on as we had played this prank on him so many times. As my brother knocked on the door and knelt to light the newspaper, the neighbour opened the door in a flash, grabbed my brother by the scruff of his neck and pulled him indoors! I saw the horror on my brother's face as he screamed out for my dad's help which was never coming. Being the eldest brother, you'd think I would have made a valiant attempt to rescue him but sadly, that's not me. As soon as I heard his scream, my friends and I ran like the wind without looking back. To this day, it is a tale that still makes me laugh uncontrollably.

I never really had problems at primary school. It was a small school. I think I was a helpful kid. I was never really naughty as I didn't want to get in trouble with teachers or my parents. I avoided conflict with other kids because I was very afraid of being beaten up, although I don't remember being picked on or bullied.

I enjoyed being involved with team sports as it helped me feel that I belonged. Looking back, there were some good teachers at our school but there was one who terrified the life out of me.

This teacher was beyond strict and their rules were rarely broken. One day I remember this teacher grabbing me out of my chair by my ear and taking me to see our headmaster. To this day, I cannot recall what I had done wrong. All I know is that I was scared and I just wanted to get my work done and get the hell out of there. My mum tells me that when she found out what this teacher had done - well, let's just say that I was never pulled out of class by my ear again!

Now on to another feature of my childhood, mainly a weekend activity. I didn't always have any money for the bus fare, so this was a common thing to do and my parents ***LET*** me do it - which to this day still has me scratching my head.

It involved standing on the pavement and sticking out your thumb when cars passed by in the hope that someone would stop and give you a free ride to your destination.

This, ladies and gentlemen, is hitchhiking.

Round our way it was called 'thumbing a lift'. I wish I could tell you all about my thumbing adventures but, unfortunately, I can only remember a few.

Firstly, there are no horror stories about my hitchhiking experiences, only fond memories. I don't remember how old I was when I first did it, but I must have been in my teens. I used to walk from my house in Johnston, cross the road and take a shortcut through an alleyway that would bring me out onto St Peter's Road. Then I crossed the road and just stuck out my thumb.

There were only three places I would get to by thumbing a lift: Merlin's Bridge, Haverfordwest and Milford Haven. I would go to Merlin's Bridge and Haverfordwest on my own, but when I went to Milford Haven my friend Ricardo would join me.

Most Sundays, Ricardo and I would thumb a lift to Milford Haven Leisure Centre to go swimming. We only ever had enough for the admission price. Neither of us fancied walking the three and a half miles, so it was down to the thumb to get us there.

Ricardo was a bit older than me and the middle one of three brothers. My brother Jason was closer to him than I was, but sometimes we would camp in his back garden and we got along ok.

It was good to have a companion, especially when thumbing a lift to Milford Haven, because for some reason it was hard to get a lift there. We would stand on Milford Road, near the turning to Bulford Road, and take it in turns to 'thumb', hoping that someone would stop.

Sometimes it got to the point where we'd be thinking that if we didn't get a lift soon the pool would close! Yet we never thought about walking. Eventually, someone would stop and give us a lift.

Getting a lift back was a lot quicker once we'd found the perfect place to stand, which was by my school. It was a good half mile walk from the leisure centre, but it was worth it.

One day I was hitchhiking to Merlin's Bridge to see one of my cousins.

On this day, it wasn't long before a man stopped for me in a white Vauxhall Cavalier SRI.

Everything started off ok, until we got to the top of Pope Hill. At this point, the driver just put the accelerator pedal to the floor and off we went. I reckon he was touching 120mph going down Dredgeman Hill. I was shitting myself!

Eventually, we got to Merlin's Bridge and as I got out of his car, I remember being a bit paralysed. Not able to say anything to him, I just put up my hand to indicate a 'thank you'. By the time I rolled up to my cousin's door, I was somewhat back in control.

A short walk led me into the woods where I met a few more of my cousins. It was a day I'll never forget. There were enough of us to make two teams and one had to find the other. It was a bit like paintballing today, but without the paint. We had pellet guns, which were legal and great fun.

The team I was in had to hide first, so off we went into the woods. As we spread out, I didn't feel nervous. There was nothing that I thought would scare me. It would have been a different story if it had been dark. In fact, there would have been no story, because I wouldn't have gone into the woods.

It was early afternoon, the light was good, and more importantly I felt good. Something inside me just clicked and I made it my mission that they were never going to find me.

To succeed at this, I had to think quickly. I decided to be like John Rambo, a character from the movie *First Blood* played by Sylvester Stallone. He was an ex-army veteran who escaped from a brutal local sheriff and ended up in some woods where his survival instincts kicked in.

In one scene, he smothered his face and arms with war paint and snapped branches off trees to put down his back and camouflage himself. When I came across some mud and branches, I didn't hesitate to do the same. I was now John Rambo Junior. I made my way to the top of an embankment. Thanks to my camouflage, I watched the other team walk straight past me. I had done it. I had completely fooled them. I had only been about two feet away from them.

I waited a short time before I made my move and headed towards the team who were doing the looking. I was doing so well. Then I made a schoolboy error and got too cocky. Just as I was coming towards an open part of the wood, my cousin saw me! He had his pellet gun pointed at me and just as I turned away yelling at him not to point the gun at me, I feel a massive sting in my buttock. He'd only gone and shot me in my bum! Bastard! It was so painful. There was no way I could stop the tears from falling down my face. Bloody hell, that hurt. I had a massive bruise for days afterwards. He wasn't remotely apologetic. He just said: "Serves you right for being cocky", which to be fair, I was.

CHAPTER 2

Fake love, fury and a furry animal

It's the mid-1990s.

"I love you mate."

"Nah...I fucking love you mate."

Ten words followed by explosive roars from our throats that resonate through the bathroom that my mate Harry and I are in.

I'm sitting in the bath fully-clothed and he's sitting on the toilet – lid down. God knows how we ended up in the bathroom, but we've got back from our night out and the ecstasy we took more than an hour ago has fully kicked in.

'God, I am fucking loving this feeling and I fucking love my best mate', I think to myself.

My eyes feel like they've been opened again for the umpteenth time and massive waves of euphoria are crashing around my body which gives me goosebumps. I feel complete, at one with myself.

I stand up in the bath. I don't know why, but I feel compelled to do so. Suddenly, I hear the song *Big Time Sensuality* by Bjork in my head and I start singing it while strutting some sort of dickhead dance moves. Then there's Harry. He's still sitting on the toilet, his feet tapping away on the floor. My heartbeat is different. It doesn't feel like it's haemorrhaging when I'm normal.

I look at Harry. I tell him his pupils are black like a squash ball.

"So are yours," he says. His feet still beat the floor. Harry and I again lock eyes and right on cue we both say: "I fucking love you, man!"

I'm still standing up in the bath, my head tipped back, riding the superior high of taking MDMA, otherwise known as ecstasy or E. I feel incredible, invincible even. I am not even talking. I close my eyes and now I can hear the sound of waves gently crashing into me with love, comfort and excitement. I want this to last forever.

Harry then begins to have a third-rate conversation about family, friends and football which seems to have meaning but I'm pre-occupied gurning (clenching my jaw and grinding my teeth) and taking slow intakes of breath in a cathartic way of stopping myself "pilling" so quickly.

Gurning is inescapable, and my face has begun to contort extravagantly. All this comes with the territory of taking ecstasy. Suffice to say this wasn't my first time taking ecstasy, nor would it be the last.

Ecstasy. It always started off as butterflies in my stomach. I got a nervous sensation, sometimes a tiny bit of nausea, but mostly just a little nervous. Then slowly, I would begin to get a rush of chemicals flowing through my body. It felt like everything was buzzing. My limbs felt like they had music flowing through them and wanted to move and dance. I would find myself 'coming up' and that was my favourite part. The rush slowly got stronger and stronger and I would feel it up and down my body in every part of me until I was there, right there, just where I wanted to be. Just where I always wanted to be, but I didn't know it until just then.

Imagine birthdays, Christmases, the summer holidays, all the wonderful emotions that we feel at the happiest of times.

Imagine that all at the same time and all 10 times stronger. I felt so happy that I literally loved the entire world. I couldn't imagine how I had gone all this time without telling everyone how much I loved and respected them.

But it wasn't just emotional; my body carried a physical euphoria like someone had poured unadulterated bliss into every single muscle and fibre of my body. Every single bit of me was singing and energetic with life and love. It was like the ecstasy of orgasm at the very best part of it; that first, blissful, pleasurable pulsation or contraction of endorphins and serotonin.

Someone had wrapped me up in a warm blanket. I felt this unbelievable connection to other people and the world. I could face things in my life that hurt me and feel totally secure and ok to talk about them. It helped me to connect to people on a level that I never knew was possible.

I absolutely fucking loved taking MDMA and I loved everyone when I was on it! This philosophical love, this unexpected mind rush had me absolutely stunned. I would "open" my eyes and look around, surrounded by friends I loved and who loved me back. I felt my heart open to the most infinite, deepest love I could possibly imagine. It was so pure and unrestricted by my own personal problems. My brick wall came down brick by brick. I could say things shamelessly that I would have previously felt embarrassed to even think about in private. When I might previously have been treated with disdain, I was now met (or so it seemed) with another's infinite love. But there would be a heavy price to pay.

I am old enough to remember the picture of a teenage girl in a coma after taking an ecstasy tablet which was widely circulated in the media in the mid 1990s, but that was not going to stop me then. I just kept on taking it, sometimes with a lot of alcohol.

I can only remember a couple of times when I drank water after dropping E. Drinking water was the recommended way to cool down when you were dancing in hot clubs and taking ecstasy. Heatstroke was something you could suffer from if you didn't cool yourself down. Most people around me did drink water but once I drank alcohol and found that I didn't suffer with heatstroke, as I thought I would, I just carried on drinking alcohol with it.

Not even passing out and falling from top to bottom of a local nightclub's staircase while under the influence stopped me from dropping E again a few days later.

You see, one thing is for certain, I am very lucky to be alive.

I was chasing a feeling that was never, ever going to be real. It was an overwhelming feeling, like a spiritual dream, that would eventually become my nightmare.

Like many people who took E, I had a honeymoon period with the drug, which created an ardent addiction. I felt my life was so dull and boring in comparison to the loved-up, uninhibited weekends under the influence of ecstasy. I came back again and again to MDMA's allure but then I discovered that the 'enchanted pill' has a double edge and I would pay a heavy price.

Ecstasy has the reverse effects of an alcohol 'hangover'. The main consequence of the drug is the physical descent some days after taking it, which includes lethargy, exhaustion, tetchiness, loneliness and despair.

My long-term misuse of ecstasy did result in some psychological damage, especially with my mental health. I began to suffer with depression and most of the anxieties I went through as a child resurfaced with vengeance.

It was like living on the crest of a wave and then collapsing. If I had continued at the rate I was going, I doubt if I would have lived more than six months. I would have absolutely lost my marbles. Ecstasy was good at eradicating my insecurities when I took it, but longer term it also shattered my faith in myself and my self-esteem.

It is a monstrous drug and it nearly caused my downfall but, in the end, I learned a harsh lesson. Yes, partying was cool, but illicit drugs of any type, are not fashionable at all.

Some years later, my destructive addiction to alcohol and drugs would result in me being homeless and living on the streets. The path that took me from a modest but mostly very happy childhood, to the lowest rung on life's ladder is one that many others have taken – but each of us has a different journey. Talking about 'THE homeless' leads to some people imagining a stereotypical down-and-out. In fact, I have seen that ANYONE can end up without a roof over their head.

Life on the streets is tough.

For instance, one day, when my facial hair had grown quite long, I was having a shave in some public toilets in Loughborough, when a man and his son came in to use the loo. I couldn't help but notice a pair of radiant eyes staring and, me being me, I couldn't resist saying in a calm voice "Hello young man, are you going shopping with your daddy today?"

What happened next completely shattered my confidence. A furious voice snarled: "Do not talk to my son you dirty smack head, piss head or whatever you are - or the next time you speak to anyone you'll be missing some teeth!"

I fell silent. I looked into the mirror trying to distract myself from launching a defence. But I couldn't see who was in the reflection. It was as if the mirror wouldn't let me see who, or what, I'd become. This complete stranger took his judgement out on me and he got it in one. I ***WAS*** a piss head living a hand-to-mouth existence in a tent hidden by trees about a mile outside the town centre – all because of drugs and alcohol.

The following morning, I headed off to get some wood for a small fire later in the evening. I was walking in the woods when I heard rustling. I stopped and quickly hid behind the nearest tree. The rustling continued but sounded as if it was getting further away. Edging closer, I thought at first that it was a stoat but at a second glance I realised it was a ferret. A polecat. It must have got out from a nearby house, I thought.

There seemed to be a composed buoyancy about this ferret and he looked very much at home here in the woods. As I tried to take a first step towards him, he heard me and his head sprang up like a meerkat. He looked me square in the eyes with a fearless stare as if he was saying 'Who are you? What are you doing here?'

The ferret bolted towards me and I decided to go down on one knee. When he got to me, he began to sniff my shoes. Apparently intrigued by my smell, he began to circle me as if he was checking me out. I stayed still. I thought back to the ferrets I'd seen as pets and sometimes strays in my home village.

I held out the back of my hand, with my fingers turned inwards to avoid being bitten, and he came in for a smell. He sniffed my hand for what felt like ages, but was only a minute or two, and then stopped. The ferret continued to sniff around me until I took the plunge and went to pick him up. I caught him off guard and managed to hold him in a way where he couldn't use his front legs to scratch me. My heart was racing but I think it was adrenaline, not blood, racing around my body. I decided to stroke his neck, partly to make friends but also to see if there was a collar or any identification.

There was none. The ferret seemed to be enjoying the affection, as if he was used to it. As I rubbed a little bit more, I could feel that the ferret's fur was not in the best condition. There seemed to be bare patches here and there. I checked to see whether he was a Hob (male) or a Jill (female) and confirmed he was a male.

"Poor chap," I thought. "I think he may have been a stray for quite some time. He's not got a collar and he's quite thin really."

I had a soft spot for ferrets, but reluctantly, I accepted that trying to keep him would do more harm than good. So, after some more rubbing, which he obviously loved and appreciated, I decided to let him go.

It was such an emotional moment to have 'someone', albeit an animal, with me after living in isolation for so long. I knew first-hand how elegant ferrets could be and when I looked at him closely, he really had an arresting face with amazing sharp brown eyes, just like my own polecat many years ago. I'd taken a shine to him and part of me was disappointed to let him go. I hadn't cried for a long time before finding this ferret, but in my disappointment the tears fell for almost an hour after I let him go.

I'd grown up around ferrets for most of my life and my memories were fond ones. My dad always had lots of ferrets and we often went 'ferreting' especially in the winter. I suppose the one that held the most intense memories for me was my first ferret. I called him Pole. When he was born, I took to him straight away. As soon as he could be weaned off his mum, my dad bought me a nice hutch for him and I made it into a palace for him, his own ferret bachelor pad! I handled him every day, putting up with the little nips he would give every now and then. The nips hurt more than a bite. I made sure that he had clean sawdust every other day and more importantly, food and water. Pole loved his food, especially the liver he would get from a freshly-caught rabbit.

Being in such close contact with an animal that had been a big part of my life before I became homeless had begun to stir something in me - but I didn't know what it was.

CHAPTER 3

Sporting ambitions

During my time at primary school, one of my teachers had a major impact on me and I had total respect for him. Mr Roach taught me for two years before secondary school and they were the best two years I had at primary school.

He was everything that I needed. He was caring, intelligent, thoughtful and memorable. He made me believe it was important to challenge myself, even at this young age, and I accepted it. He was the first person outside my family to believe in me. I always wanted to repay his faith in me. He was the first person to see I had the ability to play sport and he gave me the confidence to pursue it.

When I was 15 there was a cricket tournament organised by Wrigley's, the chewing gum company. Pembrokeshire County had just picked their U17s cricket team and I hadn't been picked. I was gutted. I thought I'd done enough to get in. The upside, though, was being asked to captain the Wrigley's team to play against them.

As I walked out on to the pitch, I could see a man I thought I recognised and as I got closer, I realised that it was Mr Roach! He was one of the umpires for the game and seeing him there made my day. What was even better was that he was umpiring from the end where I was bowling. Primary school had come and gone but he knew I had some talent and he was very generous to me when I was bowling.

'Pitch it up', 'Too short' and 'That's the line to bowl' were phrases softly uttered to me. He didn't have to do that. It gave me the confidence I needed, and I ended up taking three wickets in a five or six over spell. In your face, Pembrokeshire County!

Before long, it was time to go to secondary school and I felt weakened.

As a collective, my cousins and I were close and there were only a few of them coming to my school. I spent a year at Milford Haven Central School before going to the new comprehensive school.

I had one, possibly two, friends - but nobody took me in and taught me how to be welcomed. I used to look on in shock at the teenage smokers.

I enjoyed learning but if I wasn't playing sport then I would always look forward to getting back home and into my bedroom.

Being the oldest I had my own bedroom. Well, more like a box room. It didn't matter because it was a place where I could vanish, feel safe, dream and sometimes cry. In my room I found peace.

My world was starting to revolve around sport, so it was a relief to have a park nearby with goals up. My dream was to be a professional footballer. My first memory of football was seeing Ian Rush on TV.

Ian Rush was Wales' top striker at the time and played for Liverpool, so that made Liverpool my team. Liverpool were the best and with players like the majestic 'King' Kenny Dalglish; the tough-tackling, no-nonsense hard man Graeme Souness; the assured and magnificent Terry McDermott and the composed leader-in-the-making Ronnie Whelan in their team, who could argue against them?

As a child of the 80s, sport activities at my local park were a seasonal thing. I played football when it was football season and, in the summer, there was cricket and tennis.

Test Match Cricket, with Tony Lewis and Ray Illingworth, was on the BBC and I'll never forget the theme song, *Soul Limbo* by Booker T & the MGs, which drew me in.

Because I lived in Wales, the national team was England. It would have to be, wouldn't it? This is where I first saw Sir Ian Botham. I couldn't play for my local village team because I was too young but as soon as I watched what Sir Ian could do, man, I was hooked. He could bat, bowl and field. He could do no wrong. There was only one person I wanted to be when I started to play cricket and it was Sir Ian Botham. I played for my primary and secondary schools and it was such a good feeling to be picked on merit. I soon learned, though, that not all decisions are made on merit.

The friends and relatives that played football with me also played cricket. I remember someone had a cricket set that only ever worked on a beach. Improvisation was needed, so we'd use the old plastic milk crates, the ones that could hold about 24 bottles, for stumps. There were times when maybe 20 of us would turn up and at other times only four of us and then I used to do a lot of running for the ball.

For some reason, I never really got into tennis. It was just something to do when Wimbledon was on the telly. I do remember when Boris Becker won Wimbledon in 1984 for the first time aged just 17. He was awesome and so now I had someone to idolise in another sport. My mum had managed to get hold of a tennis racket from her favourite charity shop and I used to practice the Becker serve a lot.

Along with a football and cricket pitch, my local park had concrete tennis courts which were well maintained. There was a small charge to use them and, again, the number of people who turned up defined how long the games would last. My friends and I would take turns being ball boy. After a while though, I realised that tennis wasn't going to be for me and my summer sport was always going to be cricket.

The strangest thing about these games with friends and family was just how honest we were. There was never an independent referee or umpire. We all played in the way we were taught - in the spirit of the game. My mates and I had disagreements, but it never boiled over into a fight. You had to accept a decision you disagreed with, and carry on. None of us ever cheated in these games. I played hard just like everybody else. Parents didn't need to get involved. We all turned up and played competitively - win, lose or draw.

I would have played football all day and night, if I could. I would have taken a ball to bed with me. As soon as I woke up, I would think about football. Football offered me the prospect of glory and happiness and the opportunity to escape from the ordinary life of growing up in a small Welsh village.

My mum loves to tell me about when I was three and she and my dad took me and my middle brother to a local farm. I found a football and started kicking it around. When the farmer noticed me, he gasped: "Well I never! If that boy doesn't grow up to play football then I will eat my hat!" Sadly, I never got to see him eat his hat.

When I was nine, I got my chance to play football for my local team and I still remember that amazing feeling. Being picked for the first time and putting on my kit was the greatest feeling ever. This was my time to show Ian Rush how it was done. That feeling stayed with me throughout my playing career and I would always have a wry smile every time I put my shirt on.

My first season came and went quickly and I was glad to see the back of it. It was a disastrous season. Being heavily beaten in most of the games wasn't part of the deal. I remember our manager trying to introduce some new drills into our weekly training session. I suppose he was only trying to develop new ideas in us. This would be my last season at U11s as our next challenge would be U12s.

By the time I was in my mid-teens I was pretty much playing football every day. Saturday mornings, though, was match time. Kick-off was at 10.30am and when I got the chance to play for Johnston 2nd team, my second match of the day would kick-off at 3pm.

I had really got the football bug. Football was more than just a game on Saturday; it started to become my everything. I took my ball and practiced and practiced until I collapsed. I was quick to rush home from school, get out of my uniform, change into my favourite football jersey and blast out to play football until it was dark, only taking a break for tea.

I would wolf food down in record time, always thinking at the back of my mind that I might miss something. Indigestion was never considered as I re-joined the game still chomping the remnants of meals such as toad in the hole!

Games like world cup singles and doubles, whoever misses goes in goal next, and heads and volleys were my favourites. Phrases such as 'next goal wins' and 'no poaching' were common in the games I played. My mum and dad used to tell me these would be the best times of my life. I played football every hour that God sent with my family and friends on the grasslands and pitches, making up our own games and our own rules. There was no-one watching, except the other players.

It really was the time of my life. We would take off our jumpers to use them for goalposts and we would pick sides according to the colour of whatever replica football shirts we were wearing. If we couldn't match the colours, then one team would play with no shirts. So many times, I look back at these games I played when I was a kid and realise now, I was honing my technique without thinking, coaching myself. I wanted to find a way to beat my pals while still having unbelievable fun. Some of the matches were less meaningful; some of them meant ***everything.***

I lived on a street called The Close. Other streets in our village were Glebelands, Hillcroft and Fairview, to name a few. I have forgotten how it came about but it was agreed that we would organise a match that pitted street against street.

Date, time, venue and selections would be by word-of-mouth. The teams mostly consisted of players who were already playing for our village side, so I knew that some people were going to be good. There were also players who were my family which wasn't difficult because I was related to most of the village! This is where it got a little feisty.

I had a very close relationship with most family members who played in these games. We all just seemed to click. If we fell out with each other it wouldn't be long before we made up and all was forgotten. This would change when the street-versus-street game started. I was representing my part of the village and they were representing theirs. I wasn't going to let The Close down and neither were the others. It was war! Family had to come last because we all knew this game was going to mean more than anything. The inaugural Johnston Village cup final wasn't exactly the FA Cup final but, boy, it certainly felt like it!

I started playing as a striker, like my idol Ian Rush, because he got all the glory and was idolised by the fans. I wanted so much to be that kind of striker as well, but that all changed by chance.

It was a Saturday afternoon and I was with a group of friends on our BMXs. We were in the park where the village first team was playing a football match. My friends and I were playing who can pull the longest skid. When it came to my turn I pedalled as fast as I could, pulled my brake at the last possible moment and hey presto... I nailed it! I skidded so much that I lost my shape and fell off my bike right behind the goal being guarded by our first team goalie.

I stood up, dusted myself down and reached for my bike. It was then, in that moment, that I had a powerful urge to look up at the goal. What I saw was our goalie in the middle of his goal waving his arms and moving from side to side. Another person was putting the ball down on the penalty spot. He stepped back about five or six paces and then tried to place it to his right, which would be the goalkeeper's left.

What happened next defied any logic. Our goalie first took a step to his right, realised that he had gone the wrong way, shuffled back to the left and saved the penalty!

WOW! I was completely stunned. I kept thinking to myself... 'Did that just really happen? How the hell did he do that?' After witnessing that penalty save, I couldn't talk, walk, nothing. I was transfixed, gazing at this 'superhuman' who had just done the seemingly impossible. From that moment on, I knew what I wanted to do. I decided there and then that I was going to become a goalkeeper.

The first time I remember playing in goal was when our goalkeeper in the juniors got injured and I put the shirt on just to get some rest, as I was playing centre back at that time. The game finished, and I thought nothing of it and went back to playing in my normal position for the next game.

It was a little different, a few years later, to take up a permanent position that required hurling my body about and throwing myself, often headfirst, at the feet of players looking to get to the ball first. It is the most pressurised position on the football pitch. I understood that any moments of brilliance would often be hardly recognised, but the smallest of mistakes were noticed, remembered and criticised by my teammates for days, even weeks afterwards. For me, though, being goalkeeper was more than just standing in a goal and freezing my backside off. It was about learning, understanding and mastering the art of being the last line of defence. When I had seen what my village first team goalkeeper had done, I knew that I wanted him to teach me. So, at every opportunity, during senior training, I would ask him to coach me. Sometimes I would turn up at his house unannounced!

My mindset was positive from the word go. 'I am going to be a goalkeeper and I'm going to be an even better goalkeeper than the first team goalkeeper!' That was what I truly believed. I told my dad that I was going to play for Leicester City first before moving on to play for Liverpool. I must learn, listen and train hard - and I loved it. The more my goalkeeping mentor pushed me, the more determined I became. I was gutted when every training session ended. Over time, I would warm up with the squad and then go and do my goalkeeper training, then join the squad again to do the main training.

My dad would take me down to the park, as and when he could, and try his best to pass his knowledge on to me because he'd once played in goal too.

By the time I was 15, my team had a new manager in place ready for the U16 season. Our new coach was called Mr Price, and what an impact he had! Before his arrival, we had won some games but often we would lose heavily. I remember playing Goodwick United and losing 20-something to nil! Mr Price wasted no time in bringing new players in and we never suffered that same score line again. This was my first experience of playing with teammates from outside my village. Now I was competing with players from Haverfordwest and the surrounding areas like Camrose, Scarrowscant and Merlin's Bridge.

Mr Price, and the new players he had brought in, changed our fortunes drastically. We started winning! After some great results with my U16 team, I had found another level of confidence. There is a fine line between self-confidence and cockiness, I truly believe that. At 15, I wasn't ready to take on the footballing world, but I ***believed*** I could. This belief wasn't about being a cocky, arrogant, spotty teenager who had a few years of puberty behind him strutting round like a cockerel. Not at all. This was about me grasping the opportunities that were in front of me.

My first opportunity came when I was picked for Pembrokeshire County U16 squad. I had been recommended by my club, so I had no doubts. I was going to be the number one goalkeeper. All I had to do was prove it. I headed to the county trials. The difficulty I faced was playing in a team with people I wasn't used to playing with week in week out. You also don't get 90 minutes to make your mark at county trials.

Once I got my chance, though, everything fell into place. As a goalkeeper, communication with your defenders is vital. I had to let them know that I would be talking non-stop to them. If a cross came in and I called for it, I was coming to claim it. I made my presence known. There was a bit of talk that the goalkeeper from Tenby was odds-on to claim the goalkeeper jersey, but my confidence was sky high and I knew I was better than him and the only position he was getting was a place on the bench! Suffice to say I was selected as Pembrokeshire County's U16 goalkeeper and after four league matches we were in second place.

In between playing county games, I was still playing for Johnston U16s. The season was getting better and better with each game. Winning games felt good and our confidence was growing. By the time we played Goodwick United again, on their own turf, the tide had turned. Gone was the twenty-something-to-nil heavy defeat, in came a 2-0 win to us. Boy, that felt good.

The same momentum swing happened against Hakin. Most of their players went to Milford Haven School and they held a low opinion of us, calling us 'Johnston shitty'. They used to beat us 6, 7 sometimes 8-0 and I had to go to school the following Monday, having played them on Saturday, and listen to them gloat about how shit we were.

When we did give them a pasting though, it would be a game that would open another door for me. I think we won the game 4-0. But it wasn't the clean sheet I kept which opened another door. No, it was the saves I made while playing with what turned out to be a broken capitate bone in my right hand. That is the bone located directly underneath the knuckle of the middle finger. I broke it without realising when I saved a penalty by diving to my right!

I didn't know it, but my craft, design and technology teacher Mr Davies had been watching and when I was next in his class, he asked to see me at the end of the lesson. Crikey. I didn't remember doing anything wrong so what had I done?

As it turned out, I hadn't done anything wrong. Mr Davies said that he had seen me play against Hakin and he wanted me to come and play for the school team. Wow! I hadn't seen that coming.

Unfortunately, he didn't see the cast on my injured hand, so I said that I would love to be part of the team but I was unavailable for at least four weeks. I was so excited. I couldn't wait to get my plaster off. I just wanted to play. I was out of the Johnston team as well, so I had to accept that this injury needed time to heal.

Once I had recovered from the injury, I was raring to go. I couldn't wait to get training and back to school! As I walked by my schools' sports changing rooms I glanced at the noticeboard. It had the team selection for Milford School's U17s team and right amongst the substitutes was my name! I was delighted and disappointed at the same time. Delighted because I made the team, but disappointed that I didn't get the starting position.

It was the start of something good. Being around some very good young football players can only make you a better player. When my chance did come though, I grabbed it with both hands. We had travelled up to Bangor in Wales for a semi-final match. Our starting goalkeeper was stretchered off injured and I was called upon. I hadn't been on the pitch long when I remember one of our players sliding into the penalty box and taking out the player instead of the ball. Penalty and a straight red card.

You have got to be kidding me? Without being on the pitch long, I now had to face a bloody penalty! The opposition player placed the ball on the spot and walked back a few yards. I took a deep breath in and something inside me said he was going to blast it straight down the middle. My cousin, who was on my team, came to me and said he was going to go to my right, but I just sensed he was going down the middle. The penalty was taken and I stayed in the middle and saved it. I knew it! We end up winning the game 3-2. We were in the final.

We all gathered back at the hotel and Mr Davies didn't know the result because he had gone to the hospital with the injured goalkeeper. Our captain told him the result and how I had saved a penalty. Mr Davies came to find me, and he offered his hand. While I was shaking it, he said: "Well done Enton, very well done".

We travelled home the next day. The following Monday, during the school assembly, there were announcements by our headmaster and I wasn't really listening when suddenly I heard my name. Shit. What I have done? I was racking my brains thinking 'I haven't done anything wrong'. The headmaster continued and soon I realised that he was talking about the school football team's result. To my embarrassment, the headmaster, after telling the rest of the school about my heroics, asked me to come up on stage to receive his congratulations in person.

Sadly, there was no fairy tale ending though as we ended up losing the final 3-0. I was so proud to be playing in the final knowing that it would go down in the school's history. From that moment on I went from strength to strength, staying on at the sixth form and playing for two school teams (U17s and U19s).

Finally, I had the chance to play for Johnston, albeit, the second team. This was still a big call-up. The experience gave me all the confidence I needed to try and give the manager a reason to pick me again. All I ever wanted to do was to play for Johnston. I'm a Johnston boy at heart. I did manage to get one or two games for the first team but more often, my opportunities were with the second team.

Unfortunately, my last season playing junior football was approaching. Our manager would enter us into day tournaments, which kept us playing for as long as possible. It was in one of the tournaments that I had to make the first heart-wrenching decision of my life.

I had been picked to play for the U16s at a tournament in Milford Haven. My school team-mates would be playing for their clubs so there was an extra incentive to win. All I can remember is that from the moment I made my first save in our first game, I had a feeling that this could be my tournament. There was a spark that just ignited. Our defence was rock solid. Our midfielders played like they were all conductors of an orchestra and our strikers scored at will. We ended up winning the final on penalties, where I just happened to save a few. It was because of this tournament that I experienced the thrill of being a sought-after player.

The first time I was approached to play for Milford United was when I was working on my cousin's burger van outside a Milford Haven nightclub. I don't know how they found me, but find me they did. At that time, I was adamant that I only wanted to play for Johnston and that I wouldn't leave. They said they understood but asked me to come down and meet the manager. They said, if I still felt the same afterwards then there would be no hard feelings.

I did go and meet the manager. I was more intrigued than interested and I wanted to find out who, what and why. The two men who had arrived at the burger van were men of stature within Milford football club. They had attended the tournament and seen my performance.

The manager was a decent and honest man. He knew what he wanted from the team and that made me feel wanted. He never promised me anything and told me I had to work and earn my place. I must admit, I liked his honesty from the start and what he was trying to build. To him, playing Division Five was only the start. At the end of our meeting, I shook his hand and signed for Milford.

My footballing chapter with Johnston was over. I'd like to say that it was a new beginning, but, at first, I was devastated. It was an emotional roller coaster to switch from not being wanted to being wanted. What had I done? I didn't want to play Division Five, and so on and so on. Eventually, the emotions flattened out.

I think that my first game for Milford United was against Monkton Swifts and I believe we won 3-0. As debuts go, I held my own. It's always nice for the defence to keep a clean sheet.

After about five games, I found my confidence. I was back! Playing with some very good players, we hit the front running and before long we sat pretty at the top of Division Five. After the games, I would head back to The Railway pub in Johnston and catch up with the Johnston boys.

It was interesting how quickly certain people at Johnston would try to play down my new teammates' accomplishments. We had a consecutive run of eight clean sheets and were scoring goals for fun, but instead of a small compliment, what I got was 'Well, you're only playing Division Five aren't you?'

I looked those people in the eyes and thought 'How dare you dismiss those achievements'. I would have loved my new team to play Johnston second team, who were only two divisions ahead of us at that time. I think the game would have been interesting. I finally realised that it was a waste of energy letting the comments bother me, so I just brushed them aside and continued to come to The Railway each week with another win under my belt.

My first season with Milford ended, and it had been a great first season. We made the semi-final of a cup competition and secured promotion to Division Four. Unfortunately, I still had this yearning of wanting to play for Johnston. It was my home and I stupidly made the decision to come back. What was I doing? They didn't want me. I had this belief that I could get back in the team. Unfortunately, this wasn't the case, so I once again found myself on the sidelines and feeling unworthy.

This wasn't going to be for long though as I was sought out by a semi-professional club. The call came while I was in Sileby staying with my uncle. The manager who rang me had previously managed Milford Athletic and was now the manager of Pembroke Borough. We talked and it was a resounding 'Where do I sign?' moment. Finally, here was someone who knew that I was talented enough to play at semi-pro level. I was stunned at first. Then there were waves of emotions. After our phone call ended, I was straight on the phone to my mum and dad to tell them the good news.

Unfortunately, my semi-pro career was to be taken from me before it had even really begun.

CHAPTER 4

A sliding doors moment

It was a Tuesday. I know this because I was working at the Mart, a cattlemarket in Haverfordwest, instead of going to school.

I was nearly 16 and my mum and dad would let me work there every other Tuesday, their busiest day, with one of my cousins who had a full-time job there.

This Tuesday would be one I would never forget, and it would have a massive impact on my life and my dreams of becoming a professional footballer.

My job was to usher calves into a holding pen and bring them out, one by one, into the bidding ring where the auctioneer would sell them to the highest-bidding farmer. I would have different coloured pens and mark the sold calves according to the winning farmer's colour.

I arrived at the Mart and made my way towards the chip wagon where I got a bacon roll and a cup of tea. After checking in with everyone who was working that day, I headed to the sheds where the calves were being held.

I couldn't have been there long when I was called to go and help with the cattle as someone had called in sick. No problem. Off I went. I checked in with the chargehand and explained to him that I had never worked the cattle before.

"What do I do?" I asked.

He said: "All you got to do is walk behind them and usher them with a quick voice call and they'll walk the line for you."

Brilliant, I thought. I can do this.

The chargehand gave me a wooden walking stick, which was nearly as tall as me and beautifully crafted. Together we managed to get through most of the herd. It looked as if we were all done and about to finish. Then, I noticed there was a cow that wasn't moving. The chargehand was trying his best, but this cow just would not move. The chargehand spotted me and called me over.

"Get in behind her, boy, and see if you can make her move," he said.

I did, without thinking, and as I climbed onto the metal gate and made my way into the pen, the chargehand again gave me his walking stick.

I took three steps forward and shouted, "Get up!" and whacked her on her backside.

The cow didn't move an inch. So, I motioned to do the same again only this time, as the stick landed on her backside, I saw her leg lift off the floor and heard a sound like someone had clapped their hands together.

Within seconds, my left kneecap began to throb and I realised that the cow had kicked me.

Fuck me! That hurt!

I turned around and I got out of that pen quicker than The Flash.

I rubbed my kneecap to try and ease the pain. After a few minutes, the pain subsided and I was able to go and get my day's wages.

I found out about a week later that the animal that kicked me wasn't a cow, but a bullock.

When I got home, I told mum and dad what had happened and they told me to rest my leg. So, I headed up to my room.

It had been a tough day anyway, so I was looking forward to a nice bath. With the day washed off me, and my knee feeling just a bit sore, I managed to get to sleep quite quickly.

It was some time in the early hours of the next morning that my knee began to show signs that all was not well. I remember being asleep and dreaming that my knee was being clamped and it was getting tighter and tighter.

I woke up and turned on my bedroom light to see what was happening and there it was, my left knee had tripled in size.

I managed to get to my mum and dad's bedroom door and knocked until my mum came out. I showed her my knee and when I saw my mum's face, I knew this wasn't good.

Mum tried her best to comfort me, but I knew something was seriously wrong.

All notion of time went out of the window. I have a memory of turning up at Withybush Hospital walk-in department and finally being called in to see someone.

I made my way into the assessment room. I was wearing shorts because I couldn't put a pair of jeans on. I took a seat and looked up at the nurse.

The best way to describe him would be a male version of the battleaxe Nurse Ratched from the film *One Flew Over The Cuckoo's Nest.*

He looked at my knee and gasped, which did not help at all.

I told him that I was petrified of needles, but he just brushed this aside, which really made me angry.

"I think I have fluid on the knee," I said.

"Oh! So you're the doctor now are you?" he responded, in the most sarcastic voice ever.

He took me to another room, and without my dad being there and ignoring that I was shit-scared of fucking needles, he proceeded to unpack and assemble the biggest syringe I had ever seen and told me that this would only take a minute, so I should just relax.

Relax?

'I'll do more than relax in a minute, you numpty,' I thought. 'You'll be picking me off the floor when I've fainted.'

I could feel the blood rushing to my head, I shouted for my dad who came in. I said I didn't feel well.

The nurse had no concern for me whatsoever and tried to put the needle into my knee.

"Are you giving me a local anaesthetic injection first?" I asked.

He leaned forward with the needle and said: "You don't need one. This will only take a minute."

I shouted: "I'M NOT READY!"

My dad asked him to leave for a moment. Then he stated the bloody obvious to me: "It's got to come out, so lie down."

I managed to calm myself down a little, but this was not going to go well.

Male 'Nurse Ratched' came back in and, with me gripping the hospital bed for dear life, he began to put the needle into my knee and started withdrawing the fluid.

"OH MY GOD!" I screamed.

The pain was excruciating. It felt as if my knee-cap was being pulled off.

He filled one syringe. Then another, and another until he had filled five!

Despite being in a level of pain I'd never felt before, I managed to glance at the fluid and the majority was a yellowish colour, but with red streaks that I assumed were blood.

When it was finally over, I was taken to a room where my leg was put in plaster and I was given crutches to help me walk. My dad and I finally left the hospital. Thank god for that.

On the way home, it occurred to me that I wouldn't be able to play sport, ride my bike, go swimming or play down the woods for a while. Later in the night, those thoughts hit me hard and I set off on a rollercoaster of emotions.

It was on about the third day of being in plaster that my leg suddenly felt tight and painful. It was as if there was something blocking my blood circulation and it was getting tighter by the minute.

I told my mum and then, before I knew what was happening, my dad was whisking me back to Withybush Hospital.

The first thing I thought was, 'Is my knee swollen again? If so, why? Will my knee heal? Will I need surgery? Will it swell again?'

By this point, I was in extreme pain and my whole body felt prickly. I remember looking up at the ceiling of the walk-in centre and wondering why this was happening to me.

The next thing I remember is the noise the plaster cast cutter made when the nurse cut off my plaster cast. I then saw why the pain was excruciating, my knee had trebled in size again!

This time, I completely broke down because I knew what was coming next. My dad did his best to console me, but I was devastated.

I was devastated, because there was something seriously wrong with my knee and I'd not able to do anything, never mind play football.

A lovely nurse took me into a room to start the fluid-extracting procedure again, only this time she gave me a local anaesthetic injection. This was a godsend and meant that I didn't feel anything.

Once the extracting needle was in my knee, I could sit and watch as about six syringes were filled. There was more fluid than the first time.

When the fluid finished draining, I was again taken to the plaster room and put back in plaster.

But back home, my knee just kept swelling. The next time I went back to the hospital, they just drained the fluid and never put me back in plaster again.

I still had crutches to use and was referred to an arthritis specialist. They thought my symptoms of pain, swelling, stiffness and warmth around the knee indicated rheumatoid arthritis.

I can understand why they did this, because there was a history of arthritis in our family at the time. I didn't believe for one second that I had arthritis. How could I? A cow kicked me and I ended up with arthritis?

My knee was filling up with fluid for a reason, but the reason wasn't bloody arthritis.

The next six months were hell.

Not being able to play sport, or roam outside, with my friends and family was unbearable. To add to my woes, I was travelling to a different hospital in Swansea for a dye to be inserted into my knee. Fluid would be continuously drained and at times I didn't know what time or day it was.

I was more exasperated than depressed. I was soon able to go to school part-time and I could get out and about a bit with my crutches. It wasn't ideal, but it was something.

Then I got lucky. It was decided that I should have a surgical procedure called an arthroscopy on my knee. This can identify and treat problems in the knee joint. A very small cut is made on the knee and a tiny camera called an arthroscope is inserted into the knee. This lets the surgeon see the inside of the joint on a screen.

This procedure gave me more mobility and a chance to walk without my crutches for a while, although there was no way I'd be playing sport for some time. I was gutted because I had begun developing my strength, stamina and technique. I believed I was just beginning to become a force to be reckoned with. My enthusiasm, work ethic, consistency and self-belief were coming to the fore and I was living to practice and play. My sport was my identity.

The mental pain caused by my injury, and not being able to play the sports I loved, was devastating and there was nothing I could do about it.

A year went by and my knee was no better. It just wouldn't stop filling up with fluid. I would get it drained and this was accompanied by 'Mr Physiotherapy' who I met once a fortnight because I was told I could do the exercises at home.

The rheumatoid arthritis diagnosis was firmly attached to me now, even though I still didn't believe it.

I was pulled from pillar to post by different professionals who could never quite agree with each other.

I put on weight and I was beginning to realise that my professional football dream was over and there was nothing I could do about it.

I played the 'I blame myself' game and began to descend into a self-pity party for one. My parents did their best to keep me on the straight and narrow. I did try to keep my spirits up but, man, it was hard. It was hard to put on a brave face when all I wanted to do was scream at the top of my lungs 'WHY ME?!'.

This went on for a while, right up until I met Mr Phillips. Mr Phillips is the reason I am able to play amateur sports today and he also removed my rheumatoid arthritis label forever.

He was a top orthopaedic surgeon and, somehow, I was able to get an appointment with him. Within the space of 10 minutes, he knew exactly what the problem was. After all the draining of the fluid, plaster casts, physio appointments and so on and so on, he recognised the problem.

Under the kneecap (patella) is a synovial membrane. This is the connective tissue that shapes the inner surface of the capsule of a synovial joint and produces synovial fluid which has a lubricating function, allowing the joint surfaces to efficiently move across each other.

I was a bit groggy coming round from the general anaesthetic, but I was lucid enough to understand what Mr Phillips was telling me he had done.

He had shaved my synovial membrane down to its correct size, repaired a small tear in my cartilage and given my knee a good wash out.

Within three months I was back playing my sports again. My knee was a bit sore, but I didn't care about that.

Although my dream of being a professional footballer was gone, I would be able to play semi-professionally again once my knee healed.

I sometimes wonder what would have happened if I hadn't gone to the Mart that Tuesday. In my mind I have no doubt that I would have made it to professional football.

Would I have played in the Premier League, which had just been formed? Maybe. Maybe not. One thing I know for sure is that this was a 'sliding doors' moment for me. The film *Sliding Doors* alternates between two versions of the heroine's life, one where she caught a train and one where she just missed it.

If I'd decided not to go to the Mart that day at all, or if I had stayed around the calves' pens a bit longer would I have had the knee injury?

However, I made a major decision not long after my knee operation and it would be all change and off to the next stage of my life in Leicestershire.

CHAPTER 5

First loves and a new destination

I was 17 and I think I'd probably kissed two girls.

I didn't know what it was like for a girl to smile at me - and if she did, I wouldn't have known that it meant she probably liked me.

I never got any messages from friends of a girl saying that she fancied me, nor did I get any love letters. I believed that my body was disgusting because it was nearly all covered in freckles.

I got a job working part-time at a local supermarket in Haverfordwest. I loved my job because someone had trusted in my ability to do it. It gave me a chance to interact with customers, laughing with them and finding some confidence. It worked.

Evie was my first girlfriend and the first girl I had sex with. She never knew it was my first time because I had lied to her and said I'd had sex before. I met her in a nightclub called RJ's in Haverfordwest. RJ's was the place to be on a Saturday night. I'd seen Evie look at me a few times and thought nothing of it.

Then, on my way to the toilet, she bumped into me (I now know on purpose) and I just said sorry and carried on to the toilet. It was only when I got back from the toilet and I told my football teammates about it they said: "You idiot! Go back and find her because she bloody likes you!"

Luckily, I did. I was brave enough to talk to her and she surprisingly, talked back to me. I asked her if she would like a drink and she said she would like a 'gin fizz'. Puzzled, I went to the bar and asked for this drink. I wasn't expecting what I received and the best way to describe this drink is that it came in a massive glass with gin, lemonade (not the white lemonade) lots of ice and sugar all the way around the rim of the glass!

Evie offered me a taste and from that moment on, after I had had enough of lager, 'gin fizz' was the go-to drink. We talked, we kissed (after I plucked up the courage) and we danced. Someone found me attractive and wanted to kiss me and dance with me!!

There is a song called *Dancing on My Own* by Robyn that was beautifully covered by Calum Scott and some of the lyrics go 'I'm in the corner, watching you kiss her ... I'm right over here, why can't you see me'. I was that young man, puzzled why girls couldn't see me. I did give it my all but I wasn't someone the girls would take home, until Evie saw me.

I exposed my body to her and somehow it was attractive to her. I thought I'd found perfection. Her body was beautiful, she was beautiful. I told her everything.

Before that, I used to shake my head when people talked about 'soul mates'. Poor, deluded individuals, I thought, clutching at some words that sounded pretty in a poetry book. Then, it was my turn to be in love – but within six months, it was all over.

She was the first girl to break my heart and she did it in the nightclub where we first met. I came home, and I cried and cried. Devastated and heartbroken, I managed to get in without waking my parents (or so I thought). My dad had heard my devastated tears and he came into the kitchen wearing just his underpants. He just sat with me and allowed me to hurt.

The first few weeks were hard. I did feel sorry for myself but I tried not to isolate myself. I stayed home a bit more than usual. Going out had lost its appeal. I turned up for football training and matches and gave my best, but really I just wanted to be at home in my 'den'. I didn't have many pictures of Evie and this was way before the birth of social media.

Back then, I didn't have a radio station dedicated to love songs that I could switch on to indulge in feeling sorry for myself. My answer was to listen to cassette tapes of UB40's *(I Can't Help) Falling in Love With You;* Meatloaf's *I'd Do Anything For Love (But I Won't Do That);* Roxette's *It Must Have Been Love* or my personal favourite Stevie B's *Because I Love You (The Postman Song).*

I thought I was in love with Evie but in reality, I hardly knew her. I would listen to these love songs to increase my self-pity and misery. I cried until my face felt double its normal size. I had genuinely thought she loved me too. I wondered what I'd done to the world to deserve this misery. She had dumped me like yesterday's newspaper. My heart was completely broken. The pessimist in me was renewed, the cynic had become a passionate believer.

It was during this time, just before my 18th birthday in the summer of 1994, that I found myself thinking about leaving home. I was working as an apprentice at a well-known car dealership and I found myself wanting more; a lot more. I would fall asleep thinking about moving on. It dawned on me that I had a responsibility to myself to be happy in my life and my job didn't fulfil me.

There were a few people I worked with who didn't get me and vice versa but mainly, I just got on with things. One guy took me under his wing and invested a lot of time in showing me the ropes. But despite all his efforts, I knew that I couldn't be him and do this job for the foreseeable future. The heartbreak I was going through meant it was the perfect time to get away.

Leaving family and friends was always going to be tough and although I was scared, I was also excited by the thought of gaining my freedom. There would be no restrictions. There would be no having to let my parents know where I was going. There would be no more house rules. There would be no having to eat your vegetables, no chores, no going to bed early five nights' a week because it was work the next day.

But living at home was also about being surrounded by family 24/7. It was about being taken care of when you were sick and getting some TLC from your mum who would insist on you eating some broth. It was about having someone there to help you when you needed it and being in the comfort of a home that held all the childhood memories and all the related, sweet, private moments spent with mum, dad and brothers. Those memories, good or bad, were what made leaving them behind so difficult.

I decided to make the move from Wales to England - to Leicestershire to be precise. My grandparents had said I could stay with them in Sileby until I found a job and had enough money to move out and find my own accommodation. It was to be a decision that would change my life forever.

It didn't take long to get a job. I'd been chatting on the phone to one of my uncles and he gave me some great advice about how to register with employment agencies. This paved a way for me to work with him at The Sweater Shop headquarters, in a place called Syston.

I really took to the job well, despite the warehouse manager being an absolute pain in the backside! My job was to unload yarn for the knitters who would then put it on machines that would knit and embroider the then famous Sweater Shop logo. Seven times world snooker champion Stephen Hendry was sponsored by them during my time there.

I settled in quite well with my nan and grandad. They made me feel welcome. My new life was beginning and I felt that the decision to move had been the right one. My job was going as well as expected, although working continental shifts had its ups and downs.

I was lucky because four years before I arrived in Leicestershire, the intellectual 18-25-year olds were sitting around in the daytime because unemployment was high. Britain was in recession. The perilous, low-paid job had hardly been conceived. The people who were unemployed weren't referred to as jobless, but someone who was on the 'jam roll' (dole).

The employment agency I has signed up with filled both temporary and part-time posts in warehouses. I soon realised that temporary work offered me more flexibility than a permanent position. I would work at one company for two weeks and then at another company for six weeks. I loved the flexibility and I would do my job well, and then go home.

As I was living with my grandparents, they gave me all the time I needed to find a full-time job. There was never any pressure on me to find a permanent position, although I eventually did.

Being in full-time employment meant I had disposable income. My grandad used to advise me to save for a rainy day. If only I'd listened to him. I never did save. I paid my grandparents £50 a week board and the rest of my wages were squandered on many good nights out.

My uncle had introduced me to the local football team and the welcome felt warm and inviting. I still loved my football. They all knew my dad's family quite well. I thought this would be a good opportunity to attend training sessions with the team and show them my goalkeeping qualities. It would also allow me to meet some new faces.

It was awkward at first, but over time, and usually over drinks, relationships formed, and it wasn't long before they adopted me as one of their own.

Not all training sessions were good, but the majority were, and I felt fitter as time went on. I really pushed myself to the limit and all seemed well. I was never going to get into the first team, but I was ready for the call up to the reserves if needed.

I got in from work one night and found an envelope with my name on it. This wasn't a formal letter, this was hand-delivered. Intrigued, I opened it. Inside was a letter inviting me to a signing-on night at the local working men's club with a football team called Sileby United WMC.

In the letter it said that they were a Sunday morning football team who played in the Everards Division Four League and were looking for new players of any ability to come down.

My first reaction was, 'Who? Sunday? Division Four? No! I don't want to play football on a Sunday and I'm too good for Division Four!'

I'd never played football on a Sunday. It was an alien concept to me. Senior football, in my books, was mostly played on a Saturday afternoon. Why would I want to play on a Sunday? I spoke to my uncle about it and he said there was no harm in going down to see what was on offer and take it from there. The decision to go down changed my life FOREVER.

At the working men's club, I asked where the football signing-on was being held and someone pointed me in the right direction. I was nervous, not knowing what to expect and I had my doubts. I had managed to get a drink from the bar when I heard someone call my name.

"Are you Enton?" a voice asked.

"I am," I said.

"Nice to meet you. I'm Pablo. Glad you could come down. Don't worry, we all know your family, so we'll look after you."

I walked over to where the rest of the guys were sitting and I saw a chap who was wearing a red Oasis T-shirt. I introduced myself to the gang. When the formalities were over, I said to the chap in the Oasis T-shirt: "Oasis, eh? Nice choice."

He nodded. I reached out and we shook hands.

"Enton."

"Harry."

"Nice to meet you, Harry."

"You too. Enton, is it?"

"It is."

Introductions had gone better than I'd expected and now I was feeling more relaxed. A few drinks in and we were talking about Oasis when the manager of the football team asked me to come over and chat with him.

I turned to Harry and said: "To be continued, on the Oasis front," and he gave me the head-nod of approval.

The manager explained all about the club and where he would like to take it in the future, but if I'm honest, I was being a bit arrogant. I was 18 and I knew I was a good goalkeeper and I knew where I was going. I lost interest in what he was saying but I was wise enough to be courteous and not disrespectful. There is a fine line between arrogance and confidence and I was careful not to cross it this time.

He asked me my thoughts and if I'd fancy signing on with them and I said I'd think about it - and I genuinely did. I went back to Harry and we continued our conversation, drinking pint after pint. Before we knew it, time had been called at the bar.

Another love was about to begin to dominate my life.

To start with, I drank alcohol. Cocaine, speed, amphetamines and ecstasy all came later.

From lagers, beers, ciders and spirits to wines, there are always favourites for any drinker. For the most part I drank Carling Black Label but on nights out, Kronenbourg 1664 and Grolsch Premium would be my preferences to start the evening. I schooled myself to appreciate the delicate differences between each drink. Kronenbourg 1664 had a strong taste, while Grolsch had a crisp taste. Wines had their differences too, but I never really cared about those distinctions because, in all fairness, they were beside the point.

Years later, the cans of lager in the fridge were for show. By that stage, I kept the 'real' drink of Jack Daniels hidden in the hip flasks I used to collect. They would sit proudly on shelves high up, like ornaments. I made sure that only I could reach them and only I knew that they hid a secret stash of spirits.

In the 1990s, I was having the time of my life. Drugs and alcohol made me feel cool and outrageous and at times I'd lose chunks of time; two hours here, an hour there. Drinking and taking drugs did something to me that I couldn't do for myself, to some degree. They changed me, if only for a moment. The promise of that moment was too appealing to fight. I drank when I felt contented, and I drank when I was miserable, and I drank when I was uneasy, and I drank when I was bored.

Alcohol was becoming the most important relationship in my life. I loved how the drink made me feel, and I loved its capacity to change my focus away from my own self-consciousness and on to something else, something less tender than my own feelings.

I loved the noises of a drink: the different sounds of booze pouring into a glass, the pulling of a cork as it eases out of a bottle. I loved the formalities, the companionship of drinking with others, the warming, tender feeling of luxury and valour it gave me. I also loved the taste.

My introduction to alcohol wasn't melodramatic. I can't say it was even love at first sight. White Lightning or Ace ciders weren't around in my day, but MD 20/20 was. It was like drinking a J2O fruit drink today, and easy to forget that it contained a lot of alcohol.

I never went down the park and sat with my mates drinking back in Wales. When we were down the park, or in the woods, we'd be fishing, playing, swimming in irrigation pools, doing all sorts. Drinking just didn't appeal to me.

I never fell in with the wrong crowd in my early and mid-teens. I knew that if I did, I'd get the discipline my parents deemed fit. Football sticker books were my obsession then. This gave me another escape from my everyday life. I would run as fast as I could to the newsagents and buy as many packs of stickers as possible with my pocket money. Then, I'd just about fall over myself opening them up anticipating, praying, that I got the best team emblem, the 'shiny' sticker!

I remember the first time I got drunk. The next morning, I felt like I was going to die. I even said that I was never going to drink again! I was 15.

Once the hangover disappeared, my relationship with alcohol developed slowly. It was a pairing that lasted many years and was sometimes interrupted by time apart and loving reunions.

Anybody who's ever gone from affection for a person to outright obsession knows what I am trying to say. The connection is there, caressing your heart, and then you wake up one morning and some indescribable tide has turned and you can't go back. I need it, I want it, I love it. Alcohol has become a dominant part of who I am.

I was the guy who had four drinks to your one. It always puzzled me, when I stopped off at my local watering hole, that there would be people who could have two drinks and leave. Leave? WTF? I only left if it was to go to the corner shop and buy some more alcohol to carry on drinking at home. I never tried to hide my drinking in my early 20s. One or two of my peers were happily hell-bent on achieving alcoholic oblivion too. Comparing hangovers was par for the course. It was easy to go on a pub crawl because I was full of life. Where some people found it hard to drink at home, I found it easy because it was something new. I always prepared for a night out with six, maybe eight bottles of beer, and always opened another beer at 3am or 4am after a night of partying.

11a Swan Street, Sileby; that was my first, very own bachelor pad.

How I got there gives me no pride as I look back.

When I first moved out of my grandparents' house it was into a room in the house of a woman who worked with my uncle's wife. It was such a great feeling to finally start living independently. My time there was going well until one fateful night I came back home after a hefty session on the lash. I was very drunk, and I had bought a vindaloo from the local Indian restaurant. I intended to eat it, enjoy it and go to bed and probably suffer the shits in the morning.

Unfortunately, it did not end like that. I fell asleep on the settee to be woken next morning by an outraged lady of the house. As I tried to gather myself and act 'normally', I quickly realised that the vindaloo that I thought I'd enjoyed, was spilled all over me and her cream settee! I'm pretty sure I'd soiled myself, as well. Unsurprisingly, I was asked to leave straight away. Under the cloud of a nauseating hangover, I packed my things and left.

Now you would think I would have shown some remorse, but back then I was more aggrieved that she had dared to kick me out! I mean, it was an accident! Anyway, I needed help with my hangover, so I went to the nearest shop and bought my usual 'hair of the dog' cure to help my head, which was taking a pounding.

After this, I was taken in by my auntie for a while until I started to rent 11a Swan Street. The 'best' nights at my flat were when loads of us came back from clubbing in Loughborough and under the influence of ecstasy. Everyone was chilled and 'loved up.'

When I went out drinking locally, my last drink would usually be at around 2am. If I were out in Leicester, it would be about 3am. Somehow, I was always able to get home, continue drinking, and take more drugs.

I drank destructively. I spent an obscene amount of money on coke every weekend, consumed a shit-load of beers and spirits, dropped ecstasy, and remained up most Saturdays until 7am and still went to play football at 3pm.

Whoever wanted to come back to mine came back. I never turned anyone away. Even if some of my associates hadn't been drinking with me, they all knew they could come to mine. Why, I hear you ask? It's simple. I knew that they would have more drugs. The only drug I would not allow in my flat was heroin, because I always had this massive fear that someone would overdose.

Most people who came to my flat were, in the immortal words of The Happy Mondays, '24hr party people'. At some point, there would always be a line of coke or a spliff available, and many of us brought bottles of beer back.

No doubt about it, I had fun. Music was always playing; conversations were off the planet, and I wanted all this to last forever. The 'how good was last night?' talks with my associates were hilarious, frequent, and became repetitive. 11a Swan Street soon became THE place for the 'after-party,' and I fucking loved it.

There were times when I would only have the bare minimum of food in, usually cheese, bread, and beans - all the ingredients to make a cheese and bean toastie! These would be offered out, and when someone accepted, I always found myself rolling a 'spliff,' attempting to make cheese and beans toasties (I tipped the beans inside the bread, hoping the toastie machine would cook them!) in whatever drugged state I was in.

My living room was packed with people. It was an average-sized room, and we'd all be talking disjointed, drug-fuelled conversations that felt so genuine. The chat flowed much more naturally than it would in the daytime. We genuinely believed that we could put the world to rights! I persuaded myself this was me living, getting the most out of life.

Stubbornness and a lack of knowledge stopped me from realising that there was more to life than partying. I wanted this to go on forever. I felt amazing.

I felt a spiritual resonance with whatever music was playing. I gave many, many Liam Gallagher performances in front of people who I felt were my equals. In fact, all I was doing was pursuing inconsequential relationships that only mattered at that moment.

I remember one of my associates sitting on my toilet with a saucepan on his head, giving me a coked-up rendition of David Bowie's *Space Oddity*. Fucking hilarious at the time!

There would always be someone talking drivel, but at the time, it felt like every word was fascinating and well worth everyone's time and attention, but it wasn't. We were just dickheads on coke.

CHAPTER 6

Opening the doors to new musical influences

I have no clear recollection of when the movie *The Doors* crossed my path. I have a suspicion that Harry may have introduced me to it.

This movie, in a strange way, was the catalyst in giving me permission to buy a one-way ticket to drinking myself to death. Why? Because of Jim Morrison. He was depicted with *his* one-way ticket to oblivion and as I was already consuming copious amounts of drugs and alcohol, I gave myself permission to go out with a rock 'n' roll bang. He just raised the bar for me.

A film like Oliver Stone's *The Doors* appealed to me because of its rock culture and its sadness. What I mean is that I was already deeply occupied in creating my own patterns of drug and alcohol abuse that would ultimately prove so devastating to me and my family.

I had lost faith in myself and my relationship to the world around me. I wanted to go out like Jim Morrison did, slumped in the bathtub with a sweet, still grin on my face. Jim Morrison had died at the age of 27. I was going to die at 27. I wanted to be smiling into the face of a slow descent into the abyss, which I had decided was the most beautiful and comforting certainty of my life.

I couldn't drink in moderation. I was a person who was helpless in handling drugs or booze. For me there was no moderation, I was seeking to get high and looking for oblivion. I had a belief that going out in a blaze of cocaine and Jack Daniels was the price you paid for rock heroism. Jim Morrison was the next-level rock god; an impractical poet with an heroic brand of wisdom that could only be found by living a life of relentless excess. I was a nobody, a non-entity, but I endeavoured to become a somebody; a somebody who broke through to the other side.

My introduction to the music of The Doors came on an evening when I'd been drinking in the beer garden of a Sileby pub with about six or eight guys. One of them was Alex, the only person who always lasted the night with me at my flat when everyone would pile back to mine to continue the party.

I loved him being able to stay the pace because, at that time, he was a fucking laugh.

I was probably seven to ten pints in, with maybe three spliffs shared between us all. I needed a pick-me-up so I went to the toilet and snorted a fat line of coke. 'Fuck me! That's hit the bullseye,' I said to myself.

I walked back into the beer garden and Alex said: "You up for having a couple of spliffs at mine? My parents are away so I've got the house to myself."

"Absolutely mate," I said. "Let's hit the road, Jack."

We got to his house and he said: "I've got to shower, so go chill in my bedroom and put some music on if you like."

It was late afternoon sliding into early evening and it was already quite dark. We were both a bit tipsy and stoned but it felt manageable. I remember feelings of contentment because I was safe.

I sparked up a ready-rolled joint and took a couple of drags before Alex came in and shouted: "Fucking 'ell! Me mam and dad will kill me if they smell that, so open the fucking window will you!"

Then he took the joint off me and started puffing away. I apologised and opened the window. He calmed down and started to get changed.

With the spliff finished, Alex showered and shaved and was ready for the evening. But before we left, he grabbed a CD and put it on the player. I'd got no idea what it was but he went to turn the light off. We were both on his bed and I remember him saying: "Close your eyes and let the next 11 minutes take you wherever you want this song to take you, because it's going to be memorable."

He wasn't wrong. The song he played was *The End* by The Doors. The full version. An 11-minute masterpiece. It sounds like someone singing a stream of consciousness prose. The words gradually wear you down before beckoning you back for the climax.

The End, at that time with Alex with the right set of circumstances and some good weed, allowed my mind to be free and I saw a clear image of me as a caricature. I started laughing at what I saw, but soon stopped. The gloomy drift guided by the guitarists' sinister riff, and muddled by the singer's eerily compelling voice, was the first time I had heard a sex/death contrast and this would play a major part in my ongoing quest for death by drink.

The song finished, and the light came on. Alex and I got up from his bed, made our way to the front door and didn't say a word until we got to the pub. We didn't need to say anything. The last 11 minutes had spoken for themselves.

My first exposure to The Doors had been, to quote Jim Morrison himself, 'stoned immaculate' and has never been forgotten. Jim Morrison personified a confident kind of masculine ideal that will always seem breathtaking to me, and this was at a time when I was getting stuck in a boundless cycle of drug abuse and vacuous sex that seemed a fun, meaningful way to live my life.

I was in an empty house and I was sleeping alone so this guy coming along and singing *The End* gave me a licence for destruction, and I fucking loved it. I gained happiness and validation from that belief.

Something about music just grips me. It plays such an important part in my life.

In 1996, during the frenzied atmosphere of the Britpop insurgency, I was introduced to a club night called Brighton Beach at the University of Leicester's Student Union. It featured three rooms. Two rooms were filled with pounding 60s psychedelic soul (*Cloud Nine* by The Temptations is a classic example), Motown, Indie, Northern Soul and Britpop. The main room played everything from The Who to The Libertines, Curtis Mayfield to The Supremes, and The Stone Roses to Hendrix. I lived for nights like this.

This was an extension of the music I was exposed to by Harry's brother who also introduced me to Latin Boogaloo, 6T's Soul and Hammond Groove to name a few. He would DJ Brighton Beach from time to time, but it was when Harry and I went to his brother's backyard in Wellingborough to watch him DJ, that I changed musically. It was the start of another musical education.

Harry and I travelled down with one of his cousins. Lots of other family members and friends were there. There were a lot of kisses on cheeks with the ladies and man hugs (together with back-slapping) by the men. Greeting formalities over, I headed over to the bar to get some drinks in and saw a big British Rail sign stuck to the bottom half of the bar - and it just looked fantastic! That memory of the sign has never left me. As I write this, I still have a wry smile thinking how very quintessentially British that sign was.

There were a lot of people inside and the night was going well. I mean, I wasn't expecting anything else really. We were all getting down, dancing to one great song after another. Alcohol was going down too well, but I didn't care. I was there to get my rocks off and have a good time.

There came a time when I sat down for a little rest. I watched people making their shapes on the dance floor. There were some very good dancers; proper Northern Soul movers. It was at this point that I decided that some pharmaceutical help was needed and I motioned to Harry. I was ready to drop some ecstasy.

Back then ecstasy tablets, or Es, had a lot more purity of MDMA, so when I came under the influence of the drug I was so in tune with my surroundings that the music became really intense. I was feeling 'loved up'; I felt love and affection for the people I was with and the strangers around them.

I stood up and started walking to the dance floor and began to get straight back in my groove. I continued to drink alcohol, even though someone had told me to drink water when you take ecstasy. Fuck that! I'm not doing that.

I went to the bar and I bought two pints of lager and two 'supersonics' (gin and tonic). I drank a 'supersonic' down in one and then took the rest of the drinks with me. Lord knows how I got the drinks back in one piece. Suddenly, in no time at all, the dancing stopped, the lights came on and it was time to make our way to the exits.

Just as I was heading out, I felt someone grab my arm and tug me back. It was Harry. As I was still riding the wave of euphoria, high on ecstasy, I found it hard to grasp what Harry was saying to me. After a minute or so I finally worked out that he was saying 'house party' and I was like, 'Hell, yeah! What are we waiting for?!'

I ended up in the house of someone I'd only just met and it was packed with a good crowd. Music was playing in the background, beers and spirits were readily available, cigarettes were passed around and conversation was fruitful and mainly about music. At some point, there was an offer of cocaine which I didn't refuse. I caught up with Harry and gave him a hug and told him, 'I love you man'. Then I went to the toilet and snorted a big, fat line of cocaine. 'Holy shit that's good!'

I felt my nose tingle and it started to run ever-so slightly. I kept sniffing. The gram of cocaine didn't last long but it was having long-lasting effects. Together with the ecstasy, I felt euphoric and I wanted to dance.

As time went on, Wellingborough and eventually, Northampton, became the go-to places. The music, the people, the vibe was so different. Here I was mixing with the Boogaloo, Psychedelic, Hammond groove tribe. I wanted to be in that tribe.

The music was mystical. Hearing songs such as Darrow Fletcher's *The Pain Gets A Little Deeper* and Lonnie Youngblood's *Soul Food* (which Jimi Hendrix played on) and *Memphis Soul Stew* by King Curtis for the first time just blew me away. I couldn't wait for the next gig.

Eventually, Harry's brother got to DJ at bigger venues: The Roadmender in Lady's Lane and Soundhaus in Great Russell Street, Northampton, are two I can remember that went down a storm. The gig at Soundhaus was the first time that Harry's brother had DJ'd there. I had borrowed my grandma's video camera and recorded some of the events of that night. I think someone, somewhere, has a copy of that.

More venues were added, which meant that Harry and I attended more often. I seriously found myself thinking that maybe I should move down there. Harry ended up seeing someone from Wellingborough for a while and she said that if I was serious, I could rent her spare room for as long as I needed until I found a place of my own.

I started to look for work in and around the Wellingborough area, and I was so close to making it happen, but I had this nagging feeling that it wasn't quite right so I did not push on with the plan.

Gigs in Leicester, and another club in Northampton, came thick and fast. One of the nights in the Northampton club proved particularly memorable. Under the influence of my usual substances, I had managed to get talking and dancing with a woman. I can't for the life of me remember her name. We chatted, we drank, we danced. All was going well so far. I was invited back to her place, but I had a dilemma. Most of my money had gone on drugs and alcohol and I was down to my last £20, which to me meant a gram of coke.

I'd pretty much decided I was going back to this woman's house but she had asked me to buy a bottle of cheap champagne. She promised me that she would pay me back when we got to hers as she had some cash there.

Looking back now, in a sober and clearer mindset, I can see there was no way she was ever paying me back - but at the time, I fell for it.

I visited the toilet for a 'line for the road' and then, with a bottle of cheap fizz in hand, we made the short taxi ride back to her home. We kissed in the taxi, enough for me to recognise that there would be more to come.

She was fumbling in her handbag for her keys and eventually found them. We walked through into her kitchen where she opened her cupboard for some glasses. I got the feeling she was eager to continue drinking and, in my head, I was thinking 'I'm loving this'.

Before we got 'down and dirty', I asked her for the £20 back and her reply finally made me realise that I'd been played.

"I'm just waiting for my mum to arrive in the morning with some cash as I've just realised there is no cash in the house," she said.

Fuck me. 'You twat', I say to myself. But I could manage this in the morning so I'm not going to let it spoil the night.

There was a change in me. I was 'coke' confident now. I knew that I wasn't getting my money back, so I began to be more forward with her. I poured some cheap fizz into my glass, downed it in one and said to her: "Right, am I taking you to bed then?"

"Yeah, yeah," she said.

"My room is upstairs, on the left so go up there and wait for me," she added.

I obliged. I got naked and lay on her bed. I waited. I waited a bit more. What the fuck was taking her so long? I was getting pissed off now, so I shouted down to ask her to hurry up and she shouted back, "Just a minute".

As I continued to wait for her, I started looking in her bedside drawers and I found a big, black sex toy! Fuck me, that's big! I started messing around with it, banging it on my head, in an attempt to keep myself amused when all of a sudden she walked in.

"What you are doing with that?" she asked.

"Messing around waiting for your slow arse to arrive," I said.

She wasn't happy. Her demeanour changed. I brought out what cocaine I had left.

"Fancy a line then?"

Lines snorted, we began to get down to it when suddenly there was a knock at her door. She got up to leave. For fucks sake! I waited for what felt like about 10 minutes and my patience was wearing thin.

I went to find out what was going on and walked downstairs, naked. I saw she was talking to another woman. She told me it was her friend and asked me to put on some clothes.

I said: "I don't need to; we're all adults here."

I noticed her friend looking me up and down and I told her that she was more than welcome to join in. To my amazement, she said yes! Fucking hell! Now this just got interesting! Suffice to say, it was my first and only threesome and it was amazing what I got to do with those girls, especially with the sex toy and with what cocaine I had left.

I woke up. I turned around and I was in the bed alone. All the euphoria from last night had gone. Now I was facing a reality; the reality of no money, no phone, no drugs, no nothing. I began to panic. I was on a coke comedown as well as having a rancid hangover.

I got up, got dressed and made my way downstairs. I was no longer the confident man from last night. I was now a man who was embarrassed, weak and ashamed.

I walked into the kitchen and the first girl was the only one there. I said hello and hello was said back. I asked for some paracetamols and if there was any fizz left from last night.

'No', was the reply.

Any beer or spirits? No. Nothing.

Shit.

Shit, shit, shit.

I asked how far I was from the train station and she said, probably an hours' walk.

Fuck me. This was not good. I asked to use her phone and I managed to get Harry's brother's phone number and I rang him. I explained that I was up shit creek and I needed help.

I give her the phone and she gave him her address. Luckily for me, he knew how to get there.

The half an hour wait was excruciatingly silent. I didn't know what to say.

Luckily, my hell was over when there was a knock at the door. I was so relieved when it was Harry's brother.

In the car, I explained what happened and asked how I was going to get back home without money for the train fare. He dropped me at the station and asked if I wanted to borrow some money until I came down to the next gig. I accepted gratefully and got out of the car.

As I boarded a lunchtime train and took my seat, all the emotion left my body. Now, I felt safe. I bought four cans of lager at extortionate train prices and they started to take away the hungover feeling.

After that night, I never saw Harry's brother again. By the time the next gig came around I was in a different mindset. I was between jobs and what little money I did have was spent on cheap wine and bargain booze deals.

I never did acknowledge what he had done for me, or pay back the money he lent me. It was selfish, narcissistic and he didn't deserve it. When I borrowed the money, my priority should have been to contact him and pay him back even if it left me with no money. He had invited me into his musical family and I truly felt a part of it but in the end, I wasn't part of anything anymore. I had become a nonentity.

From 1998, I was living in Loughborough and bars and music were a major part of my life there too. I was also playing a lot of football. Through that I learned the best local bars to frequent. Every town across the country has that 'go-to' bar and Loughborough was no different. It was called Busters. Every Friday and Saturday it would be jam-packed, so you had to get there early.

Busters just about managed to accommodate everybody's musical tastes. It had two massive rooms and a cellar bar. The cellar bar was for me as it just played Northern Soul. Not all my associates were into the Northern Soul scene, so I would go into the other rooms with them, pull my hip out (a dance move reference) and spend most of the night to-ing and fro-ing between the rooms. When Busters closed, we would walk across the road to a nightclub called Krystals. It was a place where we could carry on drinking and, as and when needed, take some drugs.

I seemed to be comfortable with my own company. I used to go to a couple of watering holes that were not far away from my flat, have a few beers and play a lot of pool. I had a competitive nature, so putting down my 50p to compete against somebody that I didn't know never really bothered me. Pool has its own etiquette. Win or lose you would shake the opponent's hand, stay on the table or put down another 50p.

Over the months, new friendships were created and I was made to feel welcome. These guys took me under their wing. We drank heavily and I was dancing to a new tune. POP music. ME? Pop music! Fuck right off! But it happened. I had succumbed to the dark side of music. I'd get drunk with these guys and have such a blast. I danced to Ricky Martin's *She Bangs* on a table with some girls and a friend and loved every minute of it! I would then follow the boys over to a bar called Lloyds where the night would continue.

I would meet up with the boys most Thursday, Friday and Saturday evenings at the Warwick Arms and after a few pints we would make our way over to another pub called The Maxwells. After a few in there we would get a taxi into Loughborough town centre.

Loughborough is a university town. The pubs, clubs, bars and restaurants would not survive if it wasn't for the students and that led to special, cut-price drinks deals. Pubs and clubs always used to have offers on. On Thursday and Sunday nights most of the pubs were offering pints for £1. I mean, £1 for a pint of lager! I took *FULL* advantage of this. Thursday and Sunday night drinking was lethal, mainly because I had to work on Friday and Monday mornings.

It was bad enough having a hangover on a Saturday morning when I could just die on my bed for a couple of hours, then zombie-walk to my fridge, grab a cold can of the amber nectar and drink all over again.

Monday morning hangovers, however, were a different kettle of fish. This was because working on a Monday is the worst day. It's a shit day. The first day back after the weekend and you're expected to start off work where you finished on Friday! Jog on Mondays!

CHAPTER 7

Musical tribes and the desire to belong

People who truly appreciate music and understand that music is life, true music lovers, won't limit themselves to certain types of music because of their skin colour, their friends, or what's popular, but rather sample the best from each genre.

In the 1990s, music was an eruption of anguish, vigour, colour, dance, and emotion that has never been repeated in quite the same way. I remember Grunge/Rock (Nirvana, Smashing Pumpkins and Pearl Jam); Britpop (Oasis, Suede and Blur); Modern RnB/Urban (Faith Evans, Lauren Hill and Usher); Hip Hop/Gangsta Rap (Snoop Dogg, Dr Dre, Notorious B.I.G. and Ice Cube); girl and boy bands (Spice Girls, *NSNYC and Take That); party dance routine songs (Whigfield's *Saturday Night* & Los Del Rios' *Macarena*); upbeat party tunes (Right Said Fred's *I'm Too Sexy* and Ricky Martin's *Livin' La Vida Loca);* Eurodance (2 Unlimited, Haddaway, Corona, Scatman John and the Vengaboys) and Country (Billy Ray Cyrus, Shania Twain and Tim McGraw).

Britpop was for me and I was for Britpop. It was all about singing for my generation across Britain and Britpop brought its own style, haircuts, clothing and attitude. Bands like

Oasis, Blur, Suede, The Charlatans, The Verve, and Manic Street Preachers propelled Britpop to cult status.

The 90s were a good time to be alive in the UK and I certainly felt alive in Leicestershire. There were all genres of music and footballers you felt could be your mates. Islamic fundamentalism was something that only Salman Rushdie had to worry about - after the issuing of a fatwa in 1989 by Ayatollah Khomeini of Iran ordering Muslims to kill the novelist following publication of his book *The Satanic Verses*.

I made firm friends with the Sileby Town football boys and we would go drinking around the village pubs most weekends. Alcohol and football were like best friends. They shared good and bad memories together. Having a beer after playing football, whether you'd won, lost or drawn, was inevitable.

In just 18 months I had gone from being heartbroken and devastated at the loss of my first love to singing along to Oasis's *(What's The Story) Morning Glory?* released in August 1995. It felt like a big 'fuck you, Evie' moment to the first girl who broke my heart, which had been long overdue.

The diverse musical genres of the time, and their influence on popular culture, meant it was inevitable that a TV show like *TFI Friday* would explode onto our screens, just like its forerunner *The Word* had done.

For me, the monobrow image of the Gallagher brothers is stamped permanently across the decade. It was surely one of the oddest love affairs in music history; a pair of rascals were grasped to the hearts of so many, waving two fingers at everyone including themselves.

Oasis did something that no group since the Beatles had done; they instilled the country with their self-belief, and I was no exception. A revelation materialised inside me; singing drivel as if your life depended on it was suddenly incredibly empowering. There was something in the music that I trusted instinctively and without any doubt. It's the strength of that feeling, as well as the strength of the songs, that makes those early Oasis records stand up so well many years on. Music has changed, but you can still trust it. There was no point in analysing it, you either believed in it or you didn't. I did.

Knebworth, 1996. Noel Gallagher addresses the crowd with the immortal words: 'This is history. This is history, right here, right now' and launches headlong into *Columbia.* A song with an anthemic riff, arrogance and a thick swirl of psychedelic guitar. What the crowd is witnessing (although most are probably too wasted to realise it) is the simultaneous high point and the end of Oasis and probably, Britpop.

For four glorious years, we'd been spoiled for choice with British music, British fashion, British art. But now the whole thing was on the verge of unravelling in a haze of New Labour, copious drugs and *Be Here Now*. But, in that moment, Liam's opening salvo told you everything you needed to know in the summer of 1996, Britain was the centre of the universe.

TFI Friday was a high-spirited, light entertainment show that made its TV debut in February 1996. It was perfectly timed to be the gateway to my weekends. I was 20 at the time and this was the show I'd been waiting for. It captured my identity and who I was becoming.

For me, nobody better embodies the 90s than Chris Evans. From turning breakfast TV on its head with *The Big Breakfast,* which helped me acquire an aptitude to devise excuses as to why I was falling asleep at school, to the gameshow format of *Don't Forget Your Toothbrush,* which was like a cool *Noel's House Party* but much, much better. Then came the daddy of all his TV shows...*TFI Friday*.

The tone of Chris's shows somehow summed up the mood of the time. He made me feel part of a members' club and nothing captured the post-Madchester Britpop era quite like the riff of *The Riverboat Song* by Ocean Colour Scene. This was used as a theme tune to introduce guests as they walked the length of a walkway up the bar to be interviewed by Chris.

I lost count of the times I would walk from my kitchen to my living room over the years and sit down on my settee imitating the iconic 'TFI' walk. I was a star, and ready to be interviewed (in my head) by Chris. The show regularly featured live music, mostly from the then-popular Britpop bands.

Modelled on David Letterman's friendly style of interviewing, Chris presented a live show that often saw him forced to apologise for the behaviour of guests, which I kind of enjoyed because it was rash and arrogant. I remember looking forward to every episode, dangling on each chaotic second as the camera nose-dived above the over-enthusiastic audience.

TFI Friday became essential viewing for me. It was a TV programme I was never going to miss. To me, this show was as close to perfection as you could get. It was the first TV show to ride the feel-good wave of Britpop. It captured my spirit and mood and defined the times. Maybe it didn't fit into the 'Mary Whitehouse' world where some people lived, but who cared? I loved the show because it got my weekend off to a flying start and was haphazardly unpredictable and unmissable. I had a job where I finished on Friday mornings, so after a few hours' kip I would be up and out and ready for what I now know as 'pre-drinking'.

My afternoon consisted of visiting the village pubs for a round robin of conservative 'sherberts', waiting for my associates to arrive so we could decide what the night would entail. But, before the night took hold of me, I was back at home for 6pm ready and waiting for a TV show that was a showcase for some of the planet's most exciting pop stars.

The UK had given birth to Cool Britannia and TFI was one of its love children. I yearned to go to that mocked-up bar and pretend the famous people were my friends because I craved that celebrity rock and roll lifestyle. They all seemed to be on my wavelength, and I believed I would fit right in, especially with Chris Evans.

In my mind Chris made things look and sound cool. Listening to his Radio 1 breakfast show and watching *TFI Friday* was part of my staple diet. I was living in a defining era that was coating me in the unadulterated essence of pre-millennium lad-ism, and *TFI Friday* was the platform. It was cool listening to symphonic guitar pop while drooling over pictures of Britpop pin-up girls such as Denise van Outen.

Chris had this magical ability to make me feel that he was talking my language, especially with his taste in music and his sense of humour. He had also come from a working-class background and worked his backside off to be in front of the camera on a show he produced.

Being born in 1976 was not an ideal time to come into the world because it meant that my first exposure to music would be the 1980s.

The 1980s saw the emergence of dance music, new wave and hair metal. Disco fell out of fashion in the early years of the decade and there were other genres including Euro disco (ABBA) and dance-pop (Kylie Minogue or Bananarama) that grew and became more popular.

Putting on make-up, using hair straighteners, wearing feminine clothing and destroying the ozone layer with hairspray was never for me. What was striking was just how close music and fashion had become and how many youths embraced the artists' hairstyles and distinctive clothing. My favourite style at the time was Adam and the Ants.

I could never say that I was a fan of Adam and the Ants but when I first saw the video to *Prince Charming* it completely blew me away! I was about 12 at the time, so I'd picked up the song quite late as it had been released in 1981. It also got me in to real trouble. For some reason I decided I wanted to dress like Adam, even down to the white line across his nose. I pestered my mum every time we went into town and charity shop-shopping to buy clothes like Adam's only to be told, "No! You're not going to look like that!"

I knew my mum was never going to help me acquire the make-up needed for the white line across my face, so I had a cunning plan. Of all the things I could have come up with, there was nothing more idiotic than choosing plasters! Yes

PLASTERS, and I knew where I could get them from. There was a small petrol station that also sold household items and I'd remembered that there were plasters in boxes which (I thought) were out of sight of the cashier. I walked backwards towards them, picked them up and dropped them into the back of my jeans. I walked up to the counter and bought two eyeball chewing balls for 10p and left. I had stolen the plasters.

Mission accomplished, I could now put a plaster across my face and begin my transformation into Adam Ant. After the box of plasters was empty, I decided to go back and steal some more. This time, it was a different cashier and when I tried the same move, he clocked what I was doing. He shouted at to me to stop and I bolted towards the door and just managed to escape his clutches.

I ran home as fast as I could without stopping to look behind me. Before long there was a knock at our front door. It was the police with the cashier, who coincidently was the manager. He wasn't happy at all and he wanted me arrested. I was in trouble with both the police and my parents.

My mum had always said, for as long as I could remember, that the one thing she did not want at the house was the police. If the police did come to our door, Lord help my brothers and me. I knew that I was going to be punished and I tried to prepare myself for what was to come.

I vividly remember that we used to have a coal fire in the living room and on this occasion, it was roaring with orange and yellow flames. I was staring at them through my tears, realising that I had become a thief and it wasn't cool anymore. This was serious. The police officer talked to me and then my mum for what felt like an eternity. The police and the garage manager finally left. I was now ready to face the consequences from my parents and let's just say I saw a lot of my bedroom with a very sore bum.

Adam and the Ants aside, I never really got on board with new romanticism. It just wasn't for me. The major musical influence around me as I entered my teens was pop and Michael Jackson. He was a worldwide phenomenon and could dance on a sixpence. Girls fell in love with him and most of the boys wanted to dance like him, including me. You just can't underestimate the importance of trying to master the *Thriller* dance and the moonwalk.

I had a whole collection of remarkably bad music in my early teens - truly shocking material including an unbalanced collection of one hit wonders, which I thought were cool. My 1980s' music collection gave me a boost both mentally and emotionally. It made me feel sure of myself for the first time. It was a coming of age, so to speak. It was during this time that I realised I had a thirst for music and I wanted more.... and I got more!

Alongside the songs from Simon Bates' *Our Tune*, which my mum loved so much, I also had the wonderful exposure, through mum and dad, to what I now know as the Tamla Motown sound. This style embodied soul with a distinct pop influence. A characteristic of the Motown sound was the use of tambourines to accentuate the back beat. There were stand-out, often melodic, electric bass-guitar lines with a distinctive melodic and chord structures. I can see why this sound made such an impression on my parents.

Songs from stars including The Supremes (before they became Diana Ross and the Supremes), Martha Reeves and the Vandellas, Gladys Knight and the Pips, Marvin Gaye, Smokey Robinson, The Temptations and Stevie Wonder were played like my dad had hit the repeat button. The Stylistics were my mum's favourites, but they didn't appeal to me.

Growing up listening to the Motown sound, I felt that it was not a clear sound. It was deeper than that. The sound became spiritual, a kind of music that transcended into my young conscious mind.

When I heard *What's Going On?* by Marvin Gaye, it was a musical awakening. For the first time I was listening to the words and music, no other distractions. It was one of the most magical experiences on the planet. I can only think of a handful of songs that had a massive impact from the first time I heard them. This song had something special. The song's sombre mood was in contrast to the get-together air of the vocal. Even though I didn't understand the lyrics at the time, Marvin had a voice that was smooth without a surrendering edge. *What's Going On?* became my first anthemic song. I was also influenced by the late 80s pop/early 90s dance/hip hop movement.

I remember the first time I saw a fellow pupil's book that was a homage to Ziggy Stardust and I was fascinated. Who was this guy? Who was Ziggy Stardust? After managing to pluck up the courage to ask him, he hardly ever came up for air telling me all about this pop star. This was pivotal for me. This was the first time I saw how influential a solo artist could be on someone.

My music collection began to grow. At the time, 7" and 12" vinyl was 'in' and I had accumulated more singles than albums. They included Take That (yep...Take That), Yazz, PM Dawn, Shabba Ranks, Kriss Kross, (my middle brother and I once went to a party with our clothes on back to front!) Arrested Development, Dee-Lite, The Shamen, The Prodigy, Snap, 2 Unlimited and many more including The Stereo MC's.

One of the few albums in my collection was *Disintegration* by The Cure on cassette. This was passed on to me by my cousin Lauren, who was as mad as a box of frogs! She called herself Roberta, and made everyone call her this, because she thought she was the female version of Robert Smith. For all her eccentricities, she'll probably never know or understand just how much this album influenced me.

As good as the track *Lullaby* was, *Pictures of You* was my favourite track. My mum and dad thought there was something wrong with me and asked me what I was doing listening to this 'rubbish'. Like most of my music collection, there were many idle threats to 'chuck that rubbish in the bin'. What they, and other people, didn't understand was that this song was about a fire which broke out at Robert Smith's home. Smith was going through the ruins and came across his wallet which had pictures in it of his wife, which made the song surprisingly upbeat. The lyrics were very touching: *Screamed at the make-believe/Screamed at the sky/You finally found all your courage to let it all go* and this is sung passionately with an element of romanticism.

Most people in my home village didn't really get The Cure or Robert Smith's look. It was as if they didn't want to look beyond his appearance because they thought he deliberately wanted to record an album that was depressing. Far from it. I think it was Smith's reflection of the hopelessness he felt at the time and that resonated with me because here I was, in my mid-teens, living in a tiny Welsh village that nobody had heard of, trying to figure out who and what I was going to do with my life. This album gave me the luxury of being able to identify with Smith's hopelessness.

As the 1980s faded and the 1990s approached, I had this sense that there was going to be something big on the horizon.

April 11, 1994. Oasis released their first single, *Supersonic.*

The first time Oasis came across my radar was when I heard *Shakermaker* and it had an overwhelming effect on me. It changed my life. It was an unapologetic, unspeakably cool song. To me, it was a song that fizzed with attitude and youthful posturing that was going to define who I was.

Shakermaker had been Oasis's second single. I had missed the release of *Supersonic* but that didn't matter because when I did get to hear it, it became a rare moment. As I listened to this three-minute, archetypal Britpop song, I got the jaw-dropping-goosebumps-hairs-on-the-back-of-my-neck feeling all rolled into one. Everything just clicked.

Supersonic was not only an embodiment of certifiable nonsense poetry, (*she done it with a doctor/ on a helicopter, I know a girl called Elsa/she's into Alka-Seltzer)* but also a towering anthem about uniqueness accepted by the common people. I listened more meticulously. As the chorus of

Supersonic approaches, the bragging, lyrical graffiti makes way for a much more uncertain voice; someone who lives in the darkness and struggles to get the right words out of their mouth.

The astronomic rise of Oasis made them one of the gigantic bands to roll out of the UK. This was, in part, because Liam Gallagher acted like one of the most enormous dicks on the face of the planet and I fucking loved him for it.

That's why many people hated Oasis and it's what made me like them even more. I liked the arrogant attitudes. I liked the fighting. I liked the relentless loathing and ridiculous swagger. It was so clear. It made me think that perhaps Liam and Noel knew what it was like to be insecure people; tough on the outside, scared shitless on the inside.

Oasis had become my band and with Liam at the forefront, everything about them was dynamic. Oasis was a herd of infamous assholes, obsessive in their support of Manchester City football club. They wanted to be the biggest band in the world, and, in their minds, they did it.

In Liam Gallagher my identity was being formed. His raw power radiated around him. My eye was inexplicably drawn to him, all the time. For the first time ever as an individual, the scared shitless kid I was, began to diminish, and a young arrogant and confident young man began to grow.

In August 1994, a few months after Kurt Cobain killed himself, Oasis' debut album *Definitely Maybe* was released. I couldn't wait to get my hands on it.

Definitely Maybe offered me a message of affirmation and hope in a language of extraordinary simplicity. The lyrics talked about a passionate desire to live and implied that I could stand victorious against the 1980s nightmare that had gone before.

Oasis had a working-class background that had parallels with mine. Oasis offered me an uncharacteristic vision of fundamental positivity and a working-class vision, one originated in the commonality and community of working-class lived experience. I wanted to be Liam humming the sound of 'a council estate singing its heart out'.

I became part of a society-wide desperation to become a rock 'n' roll star and leave my workmates and community behind to chase a dream of broad-minded excess in a make-believe land of sky, sun and stars that shine. I dreamed Oasis's dreams. The difference is they were living on the ground where idealism found expressionism. I was 18 and ready to lift off into escapism. I was about to discover a drug and alcohol-fuelled lifestyle, that promised paradise but never delivered it.

Being in bed at 10pm from Thursday to Saturday was never going to happen. I wanted to fucking ***HAVE*** it and be in a hip nightclub in London with the celebrities drinking copious amount of alcohol and snorting lines of cocaine off some woman's breasts in the VIP lounge.

Music was the next phase of managing my deep insecurity and anxieties. I had escaped the first 18 years of my life and run away to Leicestershire in the hope of leaving them behind.

Little did I know that the insecurities and darkness would follow me and bite at my heels.

CHAPTER 8

Madness in Magaluf, Manchester and more

In July 2000, I had the opportunity to go to Magaluf with some new friends I had made after moving to Loughborough in 1998.

Back then Magaluf, on the Spanish island of Majorca, was like a noisy but delightful cousin. The one who lives just far enough away not to have to worry about, but would always get the drinks in at Christmas!

It was the right time for change. I'd moved to a bigger flat and I'd got a great, new, well-paid job, which involved travelling between Leicestershire and Manchester - but more of that later.

For many years I had wanted to go on holiday with friends from Sileby. We were always talking about it, but it never happened, which disappointed me.

What I came to realise was that Sileby was a village where holidays abroad were family-friendly and not 'lads on tour'. Every July, Leicestershire virtually shut down for its 'July Fortnight': a two-week break where Sileby folk took themselves (and 2.4 children if they had them) away either abroad or in the UK.

I was in my prime and I'd never been abroad. I just wanted to experience first-time flying, sun, sea, sex, sand and getting shitfaced for two weeks with like-minded people.

In Loughborough, the opportunity finally came. My flat was in an area the locals called 'Colditz'. It was a deprived area with a reputation, but the time I spent there was good.

I was 23 when I became friends with Chaz, who lived in the flat below me, after an unlikely start. My brother, his mate and I had been partying in my flat till the early hours of the morning. Chaz came up and knocked on the door and asked us to turn the music down. We apologised and did as he asked. We were pretty much off our rockers, so we hadn't realised that the music was so loud. The following morning, very hungover, I bumped into Chaz and apologised again.

Fast forward a few months, and I was in a pub called The Maxwells when I eavesdropped on a holiday conversation Chaz was having with the rest of the boys I had got to know. I waited for my moment and then asked: "Room for an extra one?" Chaz nodded and said: "If you can get £300 by this date, then you're in".

I was so excited.

The very next evening, while having a few lagers after work, I handed Chaz £300 and I was soon heading off to Magaluf with the rest of the Loughborough entourage.

During this time, I had changed my physical appearance. Gone was my indie/britpop/mod conservative look. In came a shaved head, goatee and I had put on a bit of weight. I wanted to reflect an angry, scary 'don't fuck with me' look because that was what I was feeling inside.

I was influenced by the people around me at that time, and I loved it. My confidence grew for all the wrong reasons, but it was all a façade. That wasn't who I really was. I was scary and angry because I couldn't identify and cope with my feelings. I didn't know how to truly express them so I would be sarcastic or petulant and say whatever I felt like to whoever I felt needed to hear it.

Magaluf's status as one of the most popular destinations for people to go for drinking, partying and shagging every summer was as prevalent back in 2000 as it is now. It is still associated with San Miguel vodka chasers for breakfast and sexual excess pretty much every night.

To say I was excited would be an understatement. For the first time in a long while I had saved some money, borrowed some more off my dad, and I was going to wax the lot!

It was going to be a two-week holiday and I was going to be out there for my 24th birthday. I'd been working hard and the holiday couldn't come quickly enough.

Suitcase packed and ready to go, I was picked up by one of the lads' dads in his brand-new car. The car was an automatic, but that didn't stop him from driving like it was a manual and he began to thrash it. Lo and behold - the car overheated. Luckily for us, we had managed to get close enough to the airport before we broke down.

We walked into the arrivals lounge and booked ourselves in, facing a two-hour wait before the flight. What should we do? Well, it would be rude not to have a couple of 'sherberts'. I was mindful that I didn't want to be the one who got so drunk that I wouldn't be allowed on the plane. That didn't stop two of the lads though. They just got pissed in a 'fuck you' kind of way. It was so funny watching them really going for it. At one point I thought that they would not get on the plane, but they were allowed to board. I wanted to enjoy my first flying experience and wait until I was in Magaluf before I hit the drink hard.

Like many things people do for their first time, they are over before you know it. Flying first time was no exception. It was brilliant! I'd just landed in another country and the excitement was immense. The lads had been whetting my appetite with comments like 'You're gonna love it over there', 'All those birds gagging for it', 'Partying every night', for the last few weeks - and now I was here. Let's fucking have you, Magaluf!

We arrived at our resort, Fiesta Jungla, around 6-6.30am. It was to be our home for the next two weeks. Well, I say home, it was more of a place to sleep off drunken nights.

After sorting out who was sharing with who, there was only one thing on our minds: ALCOHOL! So, we headed down looking for the nearest bar that was open - and we were in luck. Another drink and another and before long we were being ushered out of the bar as the guy running it tried to explain he needed to get some sleep ready for re-opening later in the day. Gutted. I'd got the taste now and I just wanted to continue drinking. We all headed back to our rooms and luckily, it didn't take long for me to get some shut-eye.

July 23, 2000, dawned. It was my 24th birthday. I have some recollection of how it went but one thing is certain: there was alcohol, a lot of alcohol.

The boys were good to me. They just kept topping me up - like I needed to be topped up. I was the guy who was first at the bar and last out. I'm certain that after doing a round robin of pubs, the boys went to the famous nightclub BCM. I think it was Dave Pearce or Judge Jules DJ-ing. They were the top DJs at that time. I didn't really worship DJs back then. I liked most of the dance music coming out in 2000 but that was about it. I was still an indie/funk/northern soul boy at heart.

I remember going back to our resort. I'd had so much to drink but I didn't collapse. I just carried on regardless. I'd drunk everything that was put in front of me and my brain was still transmitting information for me to drink more.

I was drunk, sitting down talking to a Welsh girl who must have realised this but chose to humour me by staying. I was really trying hard to focus on what she was saying, even closing one eye just like my dad used to. This did not deter her though and we managed some sort of conversation.

She was from Cardiff and I told her I was from Pembrokeshire. The Welsh connection worked wonders as I'd now got her interested. In my mind, our conversation was like any other normal conversation. Unfortunately, there was nothing normal about my drunk-talking. I thought I was talking normally, but in reality, it was a slurred, slow-motion gibberish tone; think Chewbacca crossed with the drunk chap Rowley Birkin off *The Fast Show!*

I was in the mood to dance so I took myself off to talk with the DJ. He did well to hear what I was saying and luckily, he had the song I wanted: The Charlatans' *The Only One I Know.* I waited, and waited, and waited until I'd completely forgotten that I'd requested a song. Then, my song came on. No, it's not my favourite song but one that's in my top 10 of all time. This song was the one that made me come to life (albeit for four minutes). I made a drunken shift toward the dance floor and I danced, the indie way. Within 30 seconds I felt spiritual. I had goosebumps and the hairs on the back of my neck woke up.

Whatever I was feeling, I was right there feeling it, right in the heart of this song. I've heard this song a thousand times but that night I was fucking transcending into indie music heaven. There were people everywhere, but it was only me on the dance floor. I closed my eyes and I began to have this vision that I was the only one there. The song finished and I went back to where I'd been sitting before, completely awash with emotion. The Welsh girl was still there.

For whatever reason, my night didn't end with me falling asleep poolside. I woke the next morning with a monumental hangover and the Welsh girl in my bed. I headed straight to the fridge where there was a cold San Miguel waiting. Fucking love you, San Miguel!

Working life in the late 1990s, and at the turn of the millennium, gave you plenty of chances.

I had lots of jobs; some would last six months, some less than three months. I always remember either walking out or not turning up. I was unable to settle, mainly because I didn't have a trade so some of the jobs I had were boring and mind-numbing. Mostly though, I had a 'fuck it switch' that snapped on.

An example of this was when I found work with a company called SJB Distribution. It no longer exists, but it was a really good job. After being there for about four or five months, two warehouse colleagues and I turned the whole warehouse around. I had an ability to use space and logistics correctly. There were just boxes and boxes of old stock collecting dust year after year, so they were the first to go.

Before I joined the company, items were being picked and despatched incorrectly, so I introduced a secondary signature. This meant a second person confirmed and signed against what the first person had already picked. In a short space of time, I managed to fit right in – but that all changed one night when England played in the Euro 2000 football championships.

I was invited to join the team from work, including managers, to watch the England game in a pub in Shepshed. Things started off well. Then they took a turn for the worse. All I can remember, as usual, is that I drank heavily. Really heavily. I couldn't tell you how much, but I know that at that time, I would have easily polished off 12-14 pints plus the usual half a dozen, double 'Supersonics' (gin and tonics).

The next morning, I woke up with a monumental hangover! I was alive. But only just.

Realisation was upon me. I made an effort to get up, but couldn't. I just lay there sprawled, my clothes and bed soaked in urine and a disgusting smell of vomit. A half-turn to my right revealed the remains of last nights' dirty kebab on the bed.

My mouth was so dry that I thought Gandhi had stuck his flip-flop in there. I felt terrible. Absolutely terrible. Somehow my mobile phone was in the bed with me and it rang. I knew who it was. It was my manager.

Manager: "Morning Enton, it's just after 11... are you coming in? We need you at work."

Me: "Can't make it in Dave, sorry. I've got the worst of all hangovers."

Manager: "So, has everyone else but they have still come in."

Me: "Sorry Dave. I can't even get up, never mind do a day's work."

Manager: "Well if you don't come in then you'll have to come and see me as this is not acceptable."

Me: "Let me save you some time on this, Dave. I ain't coming in, so do what you want. See if I care."

Manager: "Enton, there's no need to be like that. Just come on in. We are in the same boat as we don't want to be here either."

Me: "Sorry Dave, no can do, so if you want to sack me then go right ahead. I don't care. You can stick the fucking job up your arse."

I hung up.

I did manage to get up. Only because I knew what the best way to cure a hangover was – DRINK MORE ALCOHOL.

There was no shower at my flat so it was painstaking getting into the bath. I washed away the smell of stale piss and I got dressed. I had to push through and make it to the supermarket where I had enough loose change to buy a small bottle of Jack Daniels and a can of Coca-Cola.

I drank half the coke and poured the Jack Daniels into the can with the rest. Within 20 minutes I was sorted. Hangover? What hangover? I felt great again. Great enough to go back into the town centre and start drinking again. I'd just been a complete, stubborn dickhead and fucked my job off so I didn't need an excuse to feel sorry for myself because I knew who my best companion was.

On my way into town, I diverted to the cash machine and checked my bank balance. I knew I had spent a lot the night before, so I was hoping the balance would be healthy enough.

I walked into The Griffin pub and had a few there before heading down Market Street to pop into The Barley Mow.

Mum and dad had decided to move from Pembrokeshire to Leicestershire in 1995. They lived in a few different villages before settling in Loughborough towards the end of the 1990s.

On this particular day I noticed my mum was in her usual café while she was out shopping and visiting her favourite charity shop. I sat with her and she bought me a coffee. In my head I was thinking that she must be able to smell the alcohol on me but I was also asking myself why I hadn't saved some Jack Daniels to go with this coffee.

My mum knew something was up. She asked me if I was supposed to be at work and I told her what happened. Right on cue I got a phone call from one of my warehouse colleagues asking me to come into work. He said all the right things but, in my head, it was all 'ok blah blah blah' and I just flat out refused. I was not coming back and I told him not to call me again.

That was that. I never spoke to my former colleagues again. Why did I refuse to go back? Well, my head was telling me I would get the sack and all this bullshit of 'It's ok, it will be fine, just come into work' would be a ruse so that the manager could get me in just so that he could sack me and humiliate me. That was not happening.

You are not going to sack ME sunshine!

My mum chipped in and tried her best to encourage me to go back in, but my decision had been made. Mum and I went our separate ways and I headed off to a day's drinking.

I was lucky back then. I could walk out of one workplace, sign up with an employment agency and get temporary work with other companies for as long as I wanted. It was work - and I always knew I had to work. Sometimes there were full-time opportunities or temporary posts that became permanent.

After walking out on that warehouse job, and with my Magaluf holiday booked and just a few weeks away, I found what would turn out to be my best job ever.

I had been browsing through the job vacancies in our local paper, the Loughborough Echo, when I came across a vacancy for a warehouse person with some despatch experience. I made contact and was asked to come in for an interview. I smashed the interview and I was in the job before I flew out on my long-awaited holiday in the sun.

My title was quite something - Holographic Foil Inspector. This turned out to be far more than the modest-looking warehouse job that had been advertised. The job had two roles: one in the laboratory, where some chemistry elements were needed, and then packing, despatching and liaising with other partners in and out of the UK, mostly Germany and America.

I had a company car and phone for when I needed to travel to a partner company in Salford, Manchester, where the image was produced onto holographic foil using a drum reel the size of a standard bath.

My job was then to cut off a three-metre size sheet and inspect it for discrepancies using a super-strength microscope. The main errors that could crop up were small air holes, which when put under the microscope were clear to see. The next process was to pack, despatch and organise collection with our international courier partner. Job done.

I settled in very quickly.

The laboratory side of the work was a challenge, but I managed to deal with it. The travelling and logistics part of my job was where I excelled and I loved to-ing and fro-ing to Salford. I would stay at a B&B which was about a mile away from where I was working.

I got to know my fellow guests, and the family who ran the B&B, well. When I had the time, I would go football training with the son of one of the managers. It became more than a customer/staff relationship.

Fellow guests were easy to get on with and there were many late nights drinking and playing cards and snooker. I became good friends with a guy called Tony who was studying at Salford University. An opportunity arose to go out with his university friends into Manchester, which I didn't refuse. It was the most surreal night of my life at that time because I bumped (literally) into actor James Nesbitt of *Cold Feet* fame. I looked up to apologise and recognised him instantly.

He also said 'sorry' and for a split second he looked at me and said: "Don't I know you from somewhere?"

I smiled and said: "I doubt that very much, Mr Nesbitt, but thanks for humouring me!"

Selfies were not a thing back then. It wasn't the norm to ask for a photograph so you'll just have to take my word for it.

I did manage to see him again as I made my way for the exit later and he kindly gave me the head-nod of recognition.

I had many a good night drinking with Tony but that night was the best.

My company had given me a subsistence allowance and I used this for more drinking. I drank most nights at home, so this didn't stop when I was working away. I would have a basic evening meal when I got back from work and then max out my allowance with drink. If I needed to, the B&B manager was happy to open a tab for me and it would easily be a three-figure sum by the end of the week.

I also had a great relationship with the managers and staff at the foil company in Salford, including some cracking banter with one manager regarding football. He was a Man United fan and I was a Liverpool fan. He would call me 'a Scouse twat' and I would call him 'a Manc wanker', all in good humour. I would happily work late or come in early when it was needed. Everything was going swimmingly, until one day when we had to put personal feelings aside.

I had come into work in Salford a bit late. I made my way to my work station where a sample of foil had been left for me to inspect. Normal procedure. When I looked at it, I found defects within the image, so I made my way to the managers' office and told them. Their faces dropped. I didn't know it at the time, but the green light had already been given to carry on producing the foil. By the time I had made my way to the operator, almost half of the order had been produced.

I told the operator to stop production and I went to the machine and took another sample. I then made my way back to my work station and put the sample foil down next to the first sample. I asked the managers to come over and see the defect for themselves. They could see it. I told the managers that I could not give the seal of approval on the foil produced and the defect would have to be rectified before any more foil was produced. This did not go down very well.

I stood my ground and held on to my professionalism. After some tense moments, the managers had no alternative but to start the order again and luckily, the operator was able to find what had caused the defect and put it right. I stayed late that evening and worked my backside off to get the order back on track for collection.

When I arrived back at the B&B, I was so desperate for a drink that I was praying that someone would be there. Luckily, someone was and I proceeded to drink the tiredness out of me.

My days as a holographic foil inspector ended when I was made redundant due to alcohol issues.

WTF? Alcohol issues?

I mean, I recognised that I was drinking a bit more than usual but what did my boss know about my habitual use of alcohol? Why did he think that it had become a problem?

I was boiling inside, ready to give him such a verbal tirade in an attempt to defend myself - but I didn't. I knew there was no point because his mind was made up. I was out.

When all was said and done though, I do have to thank that manager for making me redundant instead of firing me.

Looking back, my drinking had escalated on a massive scale while I was in this job. On a few occasions I would finish at lunchtime and go back to the B&B, have a sandwich, a shower and be drinking by 3pm.

I took risks. I was introduced to the gorgeous single malt whisky Glenfiddich and on many occasions at the B&B I would polish off a bottle between my pints.

I was drinking heavily until the early hours most nights whether it was in Manchester, at home or in the local boozer. I would start thinking about drinking from around lunch time and I would get excited knowing how cold and refreshing the first pint was going to be.

After work in Manchester, it would be six or eight pints for starters, one pint to go with my shower and then back downstairs ready for my main and dessert.

At home in Leicestershire, after work, I would head to the pub and down plenty before heading to the supermarket to see what offers they had on beers and lagers and buy accordingly.

I would also take advantage of the 'three for £10' wine offers. I had no knowledge or understanding about wine but for that price, I was having some of that. Apologies to the wine connoisseurs among you, but this was just another way to get alcohol in my system with absolutely no appreciation for what I was consuming.

What I did learn was that I had a penchant for Jacobs Creek Chardonnay. Three bottles would be consumed while I cooked my dinner and then there would be a trip back to the boozer to finish off the night, typically with between six and eight pints.

This went on for as long as I can remember and it wasn't long before the 'shit hit the fan' at work.

I had confirmed a time and date with a courier to collect a scheduled order, so I knew when it was coming. I worked my ass off to get it ready the day before so that all I had to do was turn up at work and put my signature on the collected order. What happened next was a catalogue of failures due to my drinking. The first thing that happened was I overslept! Couldn't fucking believe it - the one day I couldn't be late.

Hungover, I got in my car (yep, way over the drink drive limit) and drove as fast as I could to get the foil company.

Shit! The courier was waiting for me. Now I was in a panic. I couldn't seem to get myself together. I was embarrassed and I just wholeheartedly apologised and began to make my way to the shipment.

As I loaded the boxes on a pallet truck, I had this horrible feeling that the order was short, because there didn't seem to be the same number of boxes as before. The shipment was short. Very short.

I racked my brains for the reason and when I inspected the breakdown on the denominations sheet, I saw the mistake I'd made. HOLY SHIT! I was fucked. This shipment had to be on a plane to America in the next hour and that wasn't going to happen.

I was sweating profusely now and beginning to feel even more hungover. I told the courier that I'd fucked up and to his credit he offered his help. I accepted at first but then realised that the shipment was not going out. I finished off the remaining shipment and re-arranged collection for the end of the day.

I told my boss what had happened, and he gave me the dreaded 'I'll see you in my office when you get back' line.

The drive home was melancholic to say the least. When I got home, I went to the off-licence and bought a bottle of Glenfiddich and drank until I passed out. I knew what was coming in the morning, so I didn't care.

I arrived at work stinking of alcohol. I walked into my boss's office and he asked me to explain what had gone wrong. I told him the truth and I was so glad that he didn't get angry or lose the plot with me as that would have got my back up.

He said because of what had happened with the recent shipment, he was going to let me go but through redundancy instead of firing me.

This, he said, was down to my work ethic and how well I had performed at my job and he didn't want me to have a sacking on my work history.

He continued to say that I had raised the bar on how the job should be done and that he was gutted that it had to end this way. He finished off by saying that the redundancy money was a chance for me to take some time off work and maybe look at getting some professional help with my drinking. I never asked how he knew.

I thanked him for giving me the opportunity. I was gutted too, really, because I had loved the job.

That was that.

I collected what belongings were on my desk and walked through the doors for the last time. There was only one place where I was going and that was the pub, to get absolutely steaming drunk!

I wasn't expecting much redundancy money so when it did come through to my bank account, I couldn't believe my eyes. Just under £4,000. Fuck me that's a lot of money! Question was, what was I going to do with it? Save some? Take my boss's advice and look after it while I get some help with my drinking which would help me get another job further down the line?

FUCK NO!! I did what I was always going to do. Hit the drink and drugs even harder! Rock 'n' Roll style!

CHAPTER 9

Falling in lust – and then love

During my time at the foil company, and before, I'd been single for quite some time, which meant I never had to worry about any responsibilities. I was my own man. As selfish as it sounds, I liked it this way. I didn't want to be in a relationship. Being single was the opportunity to live my life on my terms and not say 'sorry'. I loved being single.

That was until Sarah came along.

Sarah was a receptionist at the Leicestershire company. She was stunning: long blonde hair, slim figure, ample breasts and a very soft, beautiful face. A former air stewardess, she was just brilliant at her job. She was a very quiet woman who took everything in her stride. When I came into the office, I would say a few words and go about my day. I looked at her and I was mesmerised by her natural beauty. Most of my colleagues fancied her and, no doubt, wanted to sleep with her. I was no exception. The thought of sleeping with her was quickly put to the back of my mind as I believed she was never going to go for someone as ugly as me.

As time went on, we would have a little catch up and go about our working day. That was until I was invited to my colleague Dan's birthday party. It was at his house, which was close to my flat, so no worries about booking a taxi. I had been drinking before I arrived at Dan's, so I was ready to get my drink on. I hadn't been able to get hold of any cocaine, so I was pretty fucked off. So, I said to myself, 'I'm going to get absolutely fucking obliterated tonight.'

Dan invited me in and pointed me to where the alcohol was and told me to help myself. I was still feeling angry that I couldn't get any cocaine, so I took the anger out on drinking. Within half an hour I was on my sixth bottle of beer.

Plenty of chit chat was going on and I managed to catch up with Dan's brother Kobe. He had recently joined us at work. What was intriguing about him was his style and fashion. He had an indie/mod style similar to mine, only his was better. We had only had time to say a few words at work so this was an opportunity to get to know him a bit better.

I was on my way to get another drink and I asked him if he wanted one, and he said 'yes'. We talked for a bit and he told me he was in a band. I was so glad that there was a like-minded person to talk to and we had a long discussion about music. We really did get on well.

Before long, we were all summoned to raise our glasses, or bottles, and sing 'Happy Birthday' to Dan. As soon as we finished, Dan directed us to the dining room where there was an expensive-looking bottle of vodka waiting for us. We all happily accepted our shots and 'to Dan' was the cry.

Vodka is tasteless but a very powerful spirit. The second shot was locked and loaded and duly dispatched down the hatch. The third and fourth went down too well and after the fourth, there was only Dan and me accepting the fifth.

Within the hour, I was beginning to feel a bit legless. The alcohol I'd consumed was now beginning to win. My inner voice was laughing at me. I kept hearing 'You're fucked now, son, you've got no cocaine.'

As I made my way to find somewhere to sit, I bumped into Dan and what came out of his mouth next was just fucking unbelievable. He said, 'Want a line of coke?'

YESSSSSS!!!! FUCK YESSSSSSS!! I couldn't believe it. I snorted one small, but thick line of coke and it hit me almost instantly.

'I fucking love you, Dan.'

I walked out of the toilet and back towards the living room and there she was, Sarah, looking so gorgeous. She was almost mannequin-like. OMG! I tried to walk in a straight line towards her and say, in the best sober voice I could muster: "Hi, Sarah, how are you? How have you been?"

She responded with kind words and asked how I was doing. I couldn't stop myself saying: "I'm pretty fucked up actually" and started pissing myself laughing.

Sarah knew I was wasted, and I can't for the life of me remember if she said anything back. The next thing I remember is sitting on a settee, struggling to stay awake.

I could hear conversations, but I didn't know if I was supposed to engage in them, so I didn't. I heard my name being mentioned, but I didn't know if it was coming from my head. My name got louder, and I soon realised that the noise was coming from the side of me. I looked left and Sarah had sat down next to me. Within a short space of time, and without knowing what she was saying, I interrupted her by drunkenly stating: "I love you, Sarah."

WTF!

I. Said. I. Loved. Her.

I remember rambling on and on about how gorgeous and beautiful she was and all the drunken 'blah, blah, blah' you can imagine. Sarah handled it well (I think) and luckily, within a short space of time, somebody mentioned going into Loughborough town centre and I moved as fast as my drunken state would take me. I went outside for some fresh air. I felt completely embarrassed and I couldn't even make eye contact with Sarah. What was worse was that she was coming into town. Eventually, we all got separated and that was my cue to go. I had had enough. I walk over to the kebab house; bought my usual kebab and crawled into a taxi that got me home.

I had to go back into the office before I set off to Manchester and that meant crossing paths with Sarah. I wasn't looking forward to this. I walked through the front door and there she was on the reception desk looking as beautiful as ever. Now my heart was racing. I felt tremendously nervous and I just found enough courage to muster a 'Good morning' in her direction as I made my way to my desk.

I had to be on the road for 1pm, so after a few hours - and with everything logistically in place - I gathered the confidence to walk over to Sarah and ask for a quick chat.

I wholeheartedly apologised and made no secret of my embarrassment. I said that even though she was very attractive, I was not in LOVE with her and I hoped she could forgive me. She did. Sarah was brilliant about it and I suspect I'm not the only man who had expressed their love for her!

Not long after my drunken 'I love you' moment, there was an unexpected turn of events. Sarah seemed drawn to me. But being me, I had no clue that she bloody well fancied me. ME. I mean ME! It completely bypassed me. It all happened so quickly. I remember working late at the office one night and as I walked past reception, I saw Sarah was also working late. I walked over to her and we had a bit of a natter then suddenly, we ended up close to each other. Really close. I looked at her, she looked at me and we kissed! Like, proper kissing. I couldn't believe it. We stopped, looked at each other again and then left the office. I got in my car and drove home. Oh, my days!

Over the next few weeks, Sarah and I saw each other as and when we could. I would flit between Manchester and Loughborough, so when I was more office-bound we would meet up.

The thing was, we never declared we were exclusive, or boyfriend and girlfriend. We were both having fun. We went out for food after work and I think we both enjoyed each other's company. That was until I asked Sarah out to dinner.

I booked a table at a local pub on the way towards Kegworth called The Otter. It had a great reputation, so I made sure I booked it well in advance. I asked my dad to drop me off, which he kindly did, and we arrived with plenty of time to spare. I emotionally blackmailed my dad to stay with me until Sarah arrived. I was a nervous wreck and soon dad was telling me to slow down my drinking. I was knocking them back like there was no tomorrow. He decided to leave me to it, exiting with a final warning that I'd be pissed before Sarah had even arrived. A few minutes later, the door opened, and Sarah walked in. She looked stunning and it left me dumbfounded. She was wearing a full-body leopard print jumpsuit and as she made her way to me, I watched almost every man in the pub turn and stare at her. We kissed and I just stared at her and then it hit me, like a thunderbolt: INSECURITY! What a time for insecurity to appear. Thanks for nothing. I felt totally vulnerable, intimidated by her, inferior and unworthy. I couldn't stop myself knocking back my latest pint and saying to her: "Sorry, I can't do this." I walked out and left her there. I managed to flag down a taxi and got dropped off at my local to finish the night drinking on my own.

I woke up early the next morning. As I got ready for work, I must have practiced my excuses to Sarah in the mirror about 40 or 50 times but then it dawned on me. There was no excuse for what I had done, so I just went into work without worrying about it anymore.

I walked into work. Sarah was at her desk and I walked past her without saying anything. I should have said 'hello' at least. In my mind though, I'd done enough so I left her alone. Then, one night, she just turned up at my local. I wasn't expecting her, and it was quite the surprise. Just as I went to apologise, she stopped me and said: "Let me speak."

Then she let loose, not in an angry way, she just needed to get it off her chest and she had every right to do so.

It wasn't a happy-ever-after tale, though. Sarah and I had a whirlwind fling for about eight weeks, or so, which ended late one Sunday afternoon. We'd been out for a drink on the Saturday night, got very drunk and Sarah had stayed at mine.

I woke up and reached for a beer and managed to gaze at her for about five minutes before she woke up. We talked for a while and then, recovering after having sex three times, I just got this feeling that whatever this was, it was no more.

I asked her: "Is this the end now?"

Sarah replied: "Yes. I've had a great time getting to know you, but I just don't see this going any further."

We both just knew.

There were no hard feelings. It was a fling and the best way I can describe a fling is like having a thrilling, teenage crush, but far more fun because dinner dates, booze and sex are added to the equation.

She showered, collected her belongings and left. The rest, as they say, is history.

After I'd moved to Loughborough in 1998, Harry and I kind of went our separate ways. It was never a conscious decision, but life had taken a new turn for me.

I was finding my feet in a new part of town and we had drifted apart. I don't know why, but we just did. Then, sometime in 2002, we finally managed to catch up with each other.

I had completely forgotten that I still had Harry's number in my phone and I called it to see if it was still in use. To my surprise, and very much Harry's, he answered. We had a great catch up over the phone and I told him that I had just finished working 27 days straight in Salford and when I got back to Loughborough, I was going to nip over for a drink with him so he'd better get his liver in order.

I walked into what was probably our favourite watering hole at the time, and we gave each other a massive man hug, the one that includes the back slap! I was so glad to see him.

After getting the first round in, we just sat and talked. The beers were flowing, cigarettes were being smoked and we were in the full flow of conversation. We had so much to catch up on. I turned toward the corner where the jukebox was and began to add some of my favourite songs to this reunion.

The indie classics, rock and Northern Soul/Motown were roaring out as we made our way to the pool table. The first two frames went Harry's way, but I managed to sneak the third. I noticed a woman putting 50p on the side of the pool table to indicate that she would play the winner of the next game. I lost the fourth game and it was time for me to sit down. Just as I put my 50p on the side of the table, another woman came from nowhere and we put down our 50ps at the same time. I did the gentlemanly thing and told her she could go next if she wanted. She took up my offer and thanked me. I sat back down at the table where Harry and I had put our drinks. I noticed that the same woman had sat down on the opposite side, close to the bar. I looked long enough without staring and quickly looked away when she looked back at me. Interesting. I left it there.

Harry had won again so now it was the other woman's turn to play. Both our pint glasses were nearly empty, so I stood up to go to the bar and get a round in. This time I asked the two women if they would like a drink and they, surprisingly to me, said yes.

I walked to Harry and asked him: "Is it time for some supersonics (gin and tonics) yet?"

And he replied with one word: "ALWAYS!"

There was no turning back for me now. I was on it. I had the taste and I needed some chemical assistance. I had already sorted out my cocaine earlier and I honestly thought I'd use all of it tonight. I lost count of how many games of pool we played. They were just coming thick and fast.

The two women joined our table and all four of us were talking on first name terms. The woman I'd noticed first was called Steph and her friend was Angela.

Steph was an attractive woman, but I never thought for one second of hitting on her. I had selfish motives. I was there for a piss-up with Harry and if he wanted to go home at any point then I would do the same. Luckily for me, Harry was going nowhere and neither were Steph or Angela. It was such a blast. By now I noticed that a gram of coke had gone up my nose and I felt good.

I'd switched my drink from pints to 'supersonics' in a bid to slow down my drinking, but it only helped me to increase it.

It was hitting my cashflow because double 'supersonics' cost an absolute fortune and I was also buying a few drinks for the ladies. Money continued to be poured into the jukebox.

You just can't beat a jukebox that has the right songs on it. Songs that I have listened to at home, in the car or at work just don't sound the same as they do when you are under the influence of drugs and alcohol, in a pub, having a fantastic time.

The good thing about music is that it gets people talking. Steph and I were soon deep in conversation about music. I had to go to the toilet, so I said to her to: "To be continued" and off I went.

I didn't need to go, I just needed to snort a couple of lines. I was now about a gram and a half into my three grams. It looked like the rest was not going to last the night, so I made a phone call and bought another three grams.

I was having such a good time that the hours flew by fast. I had already consumed a lot of alcohol and snorted nearly two grams of coke, so my brain was transmitting a 'fuck it' signal again and this meant I'd just continue to drink more and snort more.

Harry and I decided to make a move and then, in a surprising turn of events, Steph suggested that we went to her house with Angela. I looked at Harry and we gave her the nod of approval. I bought some bottled Budweiser and Holsten Pils to take with us and off we went.

It was a bit of a walk to Steph's, but the fresh air helped. We walked into her living room and I followed Steph through to the kitchen to put the beers in her fridge. I asked where I could smoke, and I was directed through a conservatory into the back garden and we all sat out there supping a bottle and enjoying a cigarette. Back in the house, I was soon three bottles of beer in and my body was screaming 'no more' but my head was saying 'Fuck off, son, there always room for more!' I think Steph could see it too, but she didn't say anything.

Music was playing and surprisingly, the music was good. I asked Steph's permission to dive into her music collection. There was the usual stuff: golden oldies, 60s, 70s, Motown and a bit of heavy metal. What really intrigued me was when I came across the soundtrack to the movie *The Lost Boys*. There were not many people I knew who had this album, so I couldn't believe my eyes. I love this movie. I know pretty much 90% of the dialogue and I've lost count of how many times I've watched it. This 1980s film is a classy effort to update the vampire genre for what would now be called 'the MTV generation'. It combined Hollywood glamour with pop culture references.

Kiefer Sutherland's role as the magnetic leader of the vampires was cool and he made me feel being undead was very cool too. Jason Patrick and Corey Haim play brothers Michael and Sam. Sam quickly makes friends with a silly pair of comic book fans (the Frog brothers played by Jamison Newlander and Corey Feldman), while Michael sets his sights on pursuing local beauty Star (played by Jami Gertz).

The Lost Boys took me on an unashamedly glossy journey through vampire mythology, with a clever script packed with twists that builds to a surprisingly tense climax.

I must have drunkenly waffled at Steph about this film for ages, even telling her the most useless fact about the film (the greased-up, shirtless, saxophone player playing at the beach party used to play saxophone for Tina Turner). From what I remember, Steph was pretty cool and just allowed me to babble on. At the end of it all, we both agreed that the best two songs on *The Lost Boys* soundtrack were *Cry Little Sister* by

Gerard McMann and *I Still Believe* by Tim Capello (greased-up, shirtless, saxophone player).

I staked my claim to be DJ and I had an accepting audience. So, when it was Steph's turn, I wasn't too bothered at passing the aux cord to her because I knew I'd be listening to some good tunes.

The incredible power of music affects our moods and behaviour. Add a lot of cocaine and alcohol to the mix and music and I become lovers, walking together on a path to true divine enlightenment.

DJ-ing duties were in full swing, quality music was being played, and we all participated in a lot of talking, smoking and drinking. It felt as if none of us wanted the night to end.

Sadly, Harry and I had to say our farewells eventually. I could see Harry was struggling so we decided to make the move back to his. I felt ok and walking the short distance to Harry's gave me the bit of fresh air that I needed. As we walked into Harry's, I said to him 'one beer and a fag before bed' and he gracefully accepted.

Unfortunately, I couldn't find my cigarettes. I knew I had some because I'd bought 20 at the pub. You see, back then there was no smoking ban. You could buy cigarettes from a machine (yes, a machine!) and smoke inside a pub.

It quickly dawned on me that I had left them on Steph's garden table. So, I told Harry that I was just nipping back to get them as we would need them for the next day. I arrived at Steph's and knocked on the door. Thankfully, the door opened and I explained to her where my cigarettes were. She invited me in and we walked straight through to the garden. I noticed that her friend Angela was asleep on her sofa.

It is hard to know who initiated what, but what I can tell you is that I fancied Steph a lot and as I made my way back through her kitchen, I took one look at her, she looked at me and I went and kissed her. I was brave. She kissed me back. As I came up for a breath, I looked at her and thought to myself how right that kiss had felt. It didn't make me feel vulnerable. Kissing her was a big risk and it paid off.

The kiss was forceful and teasing but not aggressive. It was a kiss that heightened my senses. It was like a kiss you see in the movies that leaves a sense of longing. And that was me, longing to kiss her again.

Of all the things that could have come to my mind after our kiss, it was Harry! I remembered that he was waiting on me for a cigarette, so I quickly left Steph's and made my way back to Harry's.

As it turned out, there was no point in me rushing back because I found him fast asleep on his settee. I did the decent thing and left him a couple of fags on his table, locked the door and made my way back to Steph's.

We spent the rest of night together and I left the following morning with the usual hangover. That was that. I went over to Harry's and said my farewell and I headed back to Loughborough. I would not see Steph again until I turned up at her house, late at night, more than three weeks later.

CHAPTER 10

Living together and other life-changing events

For reasons unknown, and very surprising to me, I had been thinking about Steph while I was out with the Loughborough boys on another good drinking session. It was really doing my head in, so as the boys and I headed to a nightclub just after midnight I made the decision that I was going to see her.

I said to the boys: "This may backfire on me but I'm going to see a woman. See you tomorrow."

I'd had a few to drink, and maybe a gram of coke, but I wasn't wasted. I was merry. I flagged down a taxi and I was on my way to see her. The taxi pulled up outside her house. I got out, paid the driver and I waited. Then it hit me. What had seemed like a good idea now seemed like the worst idea ever.

I took a deep breath in, breathed out, and plucked up the courage to go for it. I knocked on the door, heart racing. No answer. I knocked again, this time a bit louder. My heart was still racing and my feelings were dancing with it, but for some reason I wasn't afraid. It was like an incredible, compassionate force wanted me to know that there was no reason for me to be afraid. I knew, in this moment, that this was the right thing to do.

A light came on and then the door opened. There she was, in her dressing gown. A few angry words were thrown my way, which I took on the chin, but then I was invited in.

She offered me a cup of tea and we sat down in her kitchen. I asked if I could smoke and she said yes. My offer of a cigarette was turned down and she smoked her own roll-up instead.

Luckily, her mood was ok, considering I'd just turned up unannounced and at an unruly hour. She handed me my cup of tea and I took a sip and put it down on the coaster next to her computer.

"Thank you for letting me in," I said.

"That's ok," she replied.

I continued: "I don't know where to start really but I'm going to give it a go, if that's ok with you."

"Well, you could start by telling me why I haven't heard from you for over three weeks?" she snapped.

My first thought was to lie, but I just couldn't. I wanted to lay all my cards on the table and be honest: "The reason I didn't call you was because I thought that night was just two consenting adults having sex. Over the last few weeks you have become more than that. You've been in my head a lot and, yes, I have been out drinking tonight, but I have had enough courage to come here and find out if you have been feeling the same way."

Man, I was being brave, by my standards.

I was certain that night that we had strong sexual chemistry, which is why it felt intimate, meaningful, like we had this connection to a special, bittersweet feeling.

With that off my chest, it was her turn to have her say. She didn't hold back. She said that she was disappointed and pissed off that I hadn't contacted her, but she too felt something after that night.

It felt like we talked for hours and by the time our conversation came to a natural end, I had sobered up.

We talked about a lot of things, including her children and our age difference (11 years) and how it would set tongues wagging. In all honesty, it did not bother me in the slightest.

Here was a woman who I was very attracted to both mentally and physically. She just had that something. I did not see our age gap as a problem. We had an undeniable chemistry that was obvious from the start. She had gone through a marriage that brought children into this world, so she was already more experienced than me, which is so valuable.

I wasn't the first man to date an older woman and I'm sure as hell wouldn't be the last.

It was during our conversation that I told her I wanted to see more of her. She agreed. I stayed the night again and this time we woke up together.

We started dating. I would stop at hers and she would stop at mine. We went on dates, had romantic evenings and spent a lot of time together, as new couples do.

As time went on, I got to know her children and this was a turning point in my life. As I've said before, I wanted to be single and then this woman came along and blew my single life away. It was surreal. I found that, like many women her age, she had the same spontaneous love of fun that younger women did and she wasn't the least bit afraid to act on it. Whereas a 27-year-old might not be tempted to ride a motorbike at whatever mph, she would leap at the chance to ride and off she went. Steph loved riding her motorcycle whenever she could. It was in her blood to ride bikes.

The more time we spent together, the more obvious it seemed that we should move in together but I didn't think it was that straight forward.

I noticed that I stayed at hers more than she stayed at mine. This, fundamentally, was down to her children. We must have spoken about moving in, but I can honestly say that I have no memory of how that conversation went.

Moving in with a romantic partner is a one-way ticket to adulthood. Although saying 'I love you' and getting sublimely drunk in the back garden watching the sun set is endearing, sharing a bathroom and household bills is much more real.

Once you move in with someone, you're announcing to each other that you want to settle down (to a degree) and enter the next phase of life where growing old together could happen to you, sooner rather than later.

I'd never lived with a significant other before, so I wondered what it would be like to move in with someone for the first time.

Do you change as a person, or does that person change you?

What affect do you have on the other person?

What about the children?

What happens when you want to masturbate?

I had no idea.

In the end, fate would intervene.

By Christmas 2002, I was working nights for a local plastic moulding company. It was a mundane job but the money was really good.

One morning, after I'd finished a night shift, I made my way over to the local supermarket around 7am and bought some food along with some beers and cider.

I had some weed at home so it was going to be a few 'snakebites' (lager and cider mixed together) and a couple of spliffs.

It was a freezing-cold morning and the roads and pavements were icy. I was walking along a path that had a white line down the middle marking the side where cyclists could ride.

As I got to the end of the path, it dropped a little to meet the street. The next thing I knew, I was on the floor and couldn't get up. I tried, but there was something wrong with my right foot. I couldn't move it. When I tried to lift my right foot up, it flopped to the side and the pain was excruciating.

I knew then that my foot was broken. Luckily for me, two cars stopped. I could see the women drivers making their way over to me and as they reached me, I just asked them to call 999 for an ambulance.

The ambulance arrived and with a lot of gas and air and swear words, they reset my foot and off we went to hospital.

I had broken the bottom of my tibia bone and had to have an operation to insert a metal plate.

Christmas Day 2002 was spent in hospital with my mum and dad bringing me my Christmas dinner. Steph visited me too. As I was going to be in plaster when I was released, my mum and dad said I could stay with them at weekends, which was a no-brainer. During this time, Steph stayed at my flat sometimes and my dad would drop me off at her house and we would stay there as well.

It wasn't long before my cast came off. With some physio to help me strengthen the muscles in my leg, I was soon walking without crutches.

Early in 2003 came the news that changed my life forever. Steph told me she was pregnant.

WTF!

I immediately started to panic and my head spun into places where it had never been before. Me? A father? Holy shit! Steph told me that she was keeping the baby and I didn't have to be there if I didn't want to be. But, in all honesty, I can't remember much after receiving that bombshell.

I knew that I felt something for Steph, and things were developing well between us, but we'd never had the 'let's have a baby' talk.

But that was history now. There was going to be a baby and what was I going to do about it?

Firstly, I went and told my parents. I remember that my dad was great. He gave me just enough of the advice I needed to make my own decision.

Steph and I met face to face. I composed myself and said that I wanted to be with her, so let's make this happen. The timing was not great, and there was the financial commitment to think about, but I never for one second thought about us living separately. We decided that I would move in to Steph's house with her children.

My son was born on the 27th August, 2003, by caesarean section. I remember seeing him being lifted up towards me and Steph. He had a thick head of hair and was covered in slime. After he had been cleaned up, he was brought back to us so we could share a moment before he was taken away for all the relevant newborn- baby checks.

The irony about his birth was that I was due to start a new job on that day so they were a little surprised to hear from me from the maternity ward.

Bringing my son back home was a relief. Everyone that knew us sent us something and it was great to feel the warmth of the good wishes that people sent our way.

There are lots of things to get used to when a baby arrives at home. I wanted to bottle-feed my son so Steph didn't have to use a breast pump. She didn't complain.

The best way to describe becoming a dad was like having plates spinning in my brain and trying to keep them spinning.

Unexpectedly, no matter where I was or what I was doing, I would have this fidgety awareness of my precious boy. Then there was the time spent playing and feeding, when you're aware of every glimmer of emotion on his little face, every tiny hiccup or murmur.

I know it's not in the 'baby handbook' but I used to lay my son on my bare chest where he would snuggle into my neck and fall fast asleep. One thing I do regret is that I never used to bath him. I left this to his mum. I was gripped by an irrational fear that I would drop him in the water. It's not as if he was going to drown! It was just something I was scared to do.

Family life had now officially started. Unfortunately, as the years went by, I well and truly fucked it up. Steph and I were to last four years and if I'm completely honest, Steph should have got rid of me way before that. It just goes to show how much she did love me. I can't say that the years we had together were fantastic because they weren't. Far from it.

I enjoyed many firsts with Steph and our son: first time he walked, first tooth, first words, first time at school, first time out as a family. The list could go on and on but there was always one thing in the way - my drinking.

I continued to drink at home as well as socially. Somehow, I was able to use cocaine less frequently at home, but I made up for that when I went out.

My behaviour became more erratic. At the start of our time together, I was full of hope and excitement and I thought I was special because Steph wanted to be with me. I was a loving man at heart and Steph was all that I thought mattered.

Looking back, however, I can see that what seemed like a strong relationship quickly took second place to my seriously dependent relationship with drugs and alcohol.

You see, there is no better feeling in the world than the anticipation, optimism and joy that you experience at the start of a relationship. Everything is fresh, exciting and new. Steph and I were energetic with feelings of lust, belonging and love. It felt so damn good.

Someone once told me that as a man, it's your obligation to direct a woman into deeper feelings of love, respect and attraction for you - and I looked at him and just laughed. After I stopped laughing, I asked why? He said it was because in the past, a woman was almost entirely at the mercy of a man for her survival. If you want to keep a relationship together with a woman, you have got to be able to develop her feelings of love, respect, and attraction for you over time and much of this comes down to your capability to be a considerate man in her eyes.

I understand this now but back then I just dismissed it with a 'what the fuck are you on about?' and carried on in my world. This was a world in which I caused mayhem, devastation and destruction.

My drinking and drug-taking was out of control, not that I would admit it back then. I've had plenty of time to look back now and see just how bad it was. And it was bad.

In the beginning I would drink responsibly and enjoy drinking. Drinking at home was my normal, but Steph never drank much at home. It just wasn't for her. To start with, I would drink maybe three or four nights a week but it soon escalated to every night.

I would nip in to the local working men's club every night after work and have an average of about six pints. I'd drive home, nip into the local corner shop and pick up some cans of lager ready to continue at home.

This was my weekday drinking pattern and when the weekends came, my alcohol consumption massively increased.

It got to the point where I was drinking at least 20 cans a night at home. Once I got the 'taste' for alcohol, there was no stopping me.

There were many red flag occasions regarding my drinking. The first was when I woke up in the early hours one morning because my brain had told me that four lagers I had left in the fridge just had to be consumed - there and then. I'd had a total of 16 cans only eight hours ago and I'd drunk 12 of them before bed. The thought of the remaining four was so overpowering that I got up and drank them. I fucking drank them in the space of half an hour in the middle of the night. I took myself back to bed with a smile full of satisfaction.

Another red flag was when my hands started to shake. It was a very subtle shake at the start. I'd tell myself I was just cold. Over time, even I had to accept that it was more than being cold. But I was afraid to go and see someone about it because I guessed it would have something to do with my drinking.

Instead, I became more devious. I noticed that a can of lager only took the edge off, but didn't fully stop me shaking, so I had to come up with a plan.

On the wall we had a shelf with some empty Jack Daniels hip flasks arranged on it as ornaments. Eventually, I devised a secret plan to make sure that three of them always contained about an inch and a half of Jack Daniels because I'd discovered that this was enough to stop the shakes. It was such a sly and calculating plan that, to this day, Steph does not know.

Every time I had a 'hangover' I would simply drink more alcohol.

It was not all doom and gloom for us as a couple though. There were plenty of times we went on dates and spent good times together. My parents would have my son a lot, mainly because they enjoyed having him but as a bonus he slept soundly through the night. Oh, how my son loved his sleep as a baby! This gave us our time and we would go and do relationship stuff.

Gradually though, my drinking and drug levels increased and I realise now that I had become terrifying to live with. Heavily drunk, with cocaine in my bloodstream and all my inhibitions gone, I raged for no good reason. I would completely lose all self-control and end up damaging household items like the toaster or the microwave.

On one occasion, I was so wasted, frothing at the mouth with anger but for the life of me I can't remember why. I was holding our metal kettle in my hand and hurled it at the kitchen window, which was not double glazed. It made a hideous noise as the glass smashed.

Steph and I would break up, then get back together, be ok for a while, then I'd turn again and we'd break up again. While we were 'on a break' (as defined by Ross, the character from the TV show *Friends*) I would go on all-day drink and drugs benders and suffer the consequences afterwards.

Because of the powerful attraction between us, Steph and I would inevitably be drawn back together.

Finally, my excessive drinking took its toll on our relationship. I ended up taking too many liberties. One of those was that I used to play in a pool league most Thursday evenings. It started off with both Steph and me going together but eventually I ended up going on my own. Every week, after the game had finished, I would end up back in the working men's club, playing cards. These card games lasted till 5am or 6am, and to keep me going I had to spend more money on cocaine. Three grams would just about last the night.

I had become someone Steph didn't need in her life. She loved the 'old me', the person she'd met a few years before. She didn't love or want the person I had become. And, so it ended.

I never, ever admitted I had a real problem with drugs and alcohol or accepted the importance of looking after myself. When I did realise, it was too late. The damage was already done.

I left Steph's house sometime in the last week of April 2006 and went to stay with an uncle until the time came to start my next job in Derby. For a long time, I went through some terrible guilt and shame for the hurt and pain I had caused Steph and I just couldn't forgive myself. After all the shit I had put her through, I was still in love with her when I had no right to be.

My mum kept telling me that time was a great healer and I would get through this. In time I did, but in that moment I didn't want to listen to profound, philosophical quotes.

It took a long time for me to adjust to what I had done. During this time I experienced a lot of suicidal thoughts. I vividly remember waiting for a train to Loughborough at Derby station with tears streaming down my face. I thought that if I stepped out it would be over quickly and I wouldn't have to go through all the guilt I was feeling.

Today, my relationship with Steph is ok. We only speak when we need to though. Unfortunately, now he is older, my son has decided not to see me anymore, for reasons I'm sure he will tell me in due course.

It does feel weird without him around. He turned out to be a very good footballer, like his dad, only he didn't want to play in goal. I had a good few years travelling to Leicestershire with him, watching his games before he gave it up. That was a shame because he was good and that's a footballing opinion not me being biased. I had coaches tell me how good he was.

Steph and I have both moved on to other relationships. I am glad she overcame adversity and found happiness again. It's what she deserves. I hope one day she will forgive me. It took years for me to forgive myself but it was something I finally had to do to move on.

CHAPTER 11

Kicking the habits – but heading for the streets

It was a Friday night in May, 2006. I arrived at my job as a plumber's mate in the works van with my suitcase; all 22 stone of me. I was seriously overweight.

There wasn't much in my suitcase, considering a four-year relationship had just ended. The devastation I had caused because of drugs and alcohol could all have been avoided. I had been in a downward spiral for a long time. This was the final straw.

Enough was enough.

Enton, I'm afraid you've had your last call for alcohol.

You are not welcomed by alcohol any longer!

I know that sounds silly to say, but it's the truth.

I went to work, but it was as if I wasn't there. I felt like a zombie, only this time, it wasn't because of drink or drugs. I knew why I felt like this and it was the same way I felt when I was 17 and my first girlfriend dumped me.

Oh, and there were two other crucial things to note: I had nowhere to live and I finally realised that I probably needed to seek help for my alcohol intake. Triple fucking whammy!

I finished work and with some help I managed to get a room in a pub. Yep, you read that right, a pub! There were no alternatives. I hadn't got the £1,000 it would take to privately rent - so there it was.

I walked into the room and put down my suitcase. I sat on the bed with my head in my hands thinking 'What now?'

My thoughts wrestled with each other. Should I, or should I not, get absolutely blinding drunk? That's what I used to do. When Steph and I would argue, I would throw all my toys out of my pram, spit my dummy out and head straight to the pub, get wasted and suffer the consequences under another devastating hangover.

Sadly, this was what I chose to do on my first night at the pub, and to be honest it just felt so good to do it. I just needed to stop the world for a night and just drink until I could drink no more.

Surprisingly, I slept ok. I woke up on Saturday morning with the devastating hangover I'd been expecting, but this hangover was different. I think, subconsciously, I knew that this had been my last goodbye to my life with alcohol as I knew it.

Last orders had been called and gone. I got up, showered, and then went out into the town centre, bought some paracetamols and had a fried breakfast in the local café.

Luckily, my room had a TV, so I pretty much chilled out for most of the weekend, only going out to get food when I was hungry.

When Sunday began to draw in, I decided that after work on Monday, I was going to the local walk-in health centre to talk to someone about my drinking. I must admit I was terrified. I never wanted to admit that I might have a problem, but my suspicions had grown.

The moment had arrived. As I walked in, for a split second, I thought 'What if they tell me I have a drink problem and ask me to stop drinking?'

I managed to get to the reception desk and it was quiet. I said that I wasn't injured or anything, but I was hoping to talk to someone in private about some alcohol issues.

I was asked to take a seat and told that someone would be there shortly.

While I waited, my mind was racing. What if I am an alcoholic? Will they ask me to stop? What if my pride gets in the way? I don't want to be stigmatised.

I resisted all temptation to leave and finally I was seen. A woman came over to me and asked me to follow her into a side room.

After about a 10-minute conversation, everything came out. It was never my intention, but it did. I left with some contact details for an alcohol abuse project and was told that they would probably give me the help I needed. They certainly did.

Firstly, I was informed that I couldn't just stop, I had to reduce. I didn't want a structured detox where I would be in hospital and cared for with prescribed medication. No. I didn't want that. I didn't want to be at the mercy of other people when I believed I could help myself. I was stubborn and I dug my heels in.

It was my fucking pride getting in the way. It was also because I felt I would become totally worthless. I would have to accept that alcohol had more power over me than I realised. It was abundantly clear that alcohol, more than the illicit drugs, had taken more from me than it had ever given back.

This was going to be tough and I never, ever took what had to happen lightly. If I didn't do this, I would die slowly and in agonising pain.

I took annual leave from work for a few days in preparation for this. My first withdrawal was fucking horrible. There was nothing I could do when the shaking started. I couldn't take another drink to make it go away this time. I just had to let it do its thing.

I knew relief would come, eventually. The velocity of my shaking wasn't uncontrollable, but it felt as if it was.

Then came the night sweats. My bed looked like I had soiled it again. When I wasn't shaking, I was sweating and vice versa. I had water, some over-the-counter paracetamols and Librium (which I had managed to get off 'someone who knew someone') on my bedside table ready to ingest.

I did this for three days and I seemed to get better. As the week ended, I felt surprisingly OK. I was expecting to feel much worse. I went back to work within 10 days, and no-one was any the wiser. That's what I wanted. I didn't want anyone to know. I was so relieved.

I had to buy new bedding, but otherwise I came through it pretty much unscathed. During this time, I was talking to my parents. I never told them the details, only that I had stopped drinking. So, they were none the wiser either.

I would go and stay with them on a few weekends and my mum would do my washing for me. I spent time with my dad helping him with his horses and I did my best to distract myself from drinking.

It was hard.

I faced the emotional difficulties of my relationship breakdown again, because the more I saw Steph, the more I knew I still loved her.

Unfortunately, she had moved on and was seeing someone else which, at the time, was devastating but who can blame her? Certainly not me. Seeing my son was always good and I brought him to stay with me when I could.

The first week in sobriety felt like a massive smack in the face. This was all new to me, so I knew nothing about failed attempts. The desire to go back and escape into a drugs and alcohol-induced oblivion felt virtually irresistible.

Instead of rolling up my sleeves ready for the fight, I succumbed to the lure of drugs and alcohol on two occasions: June 2006 and January 2007.

These weren't romantic reunions. The first was at a music gig and the other was when I was staying at my dad's caravan.

I never planned to drink alcohol or take drugs. It just happened without me even thinking about the consequences. I was offered a drink at the gig and still, to this day, I don't know why my brain engaged the autopilot button and said

'I'll have a pint of lager. please.' It only occurred to me what I'd done when I had drunk half of it, and then my heart sank. I realised what I had done, and that my week of withdrawal had been for nothing. In that moment I hated myself. I tried to explain it away in my head that it was OK, it was only half a pint. I can drink this moderately. Yes, things have changed now. I can finish off this pint moderately.

Drink moderately? Me? I've heard some bullshit come out of my mouth before but this one tops them all! All this 'moderate drinking bullshit' did was give me the permission I needed to drink the rest of my drink, and then go on and drink more. The more I drank, the more I wanted to drink. Drinking amplified my thirst. I needed the second drink more than the first, the fourth more than I'd needed the third and the eighth more than the seventh.

My thirst got bigger over the course of the night, so I needed to find some chemical assistance. It didn't take too long to buy some, but I might as well not have bothered because A) the cocaine I bought didn't give the hit that I was used to before and B) it smelt and tasted a bit like talcum powder! Nevertheless, I snorted it. It gave me a small lift and I drank until I couldn't drink anymore.

Looking back now, I think there were subconscious warning signs of a lapse to come. Thoughts of drinking had been brewing under the surface. My cravings in the week leading up to the gig were hard to control. I felt weakened by these cravings, which were sinister. All I wanted to do was drink and take drugs. I had the money and I couldn't stop myself, so I didn't.

Music and I have had a long love affair. Add drugs and alcohol to the mix and I ride the musical rollercoaster because it communicates a range of emotions to me.

I went to bed and slept after the gig. I woke the next morning with a cloudy hangover filled with shame but surprisingly didn't feel the need to drink alcohol to take the edge off it.

The only thing different with my second blip was that I had come back to see my parents to spend Christmas and New Year with them and see my son. There was no room in their house, so I took my dad up on his offer to stay in his caravan.

It was good to be away from the pub that was my home at the time. I started drinking soft drinks, but thoughts of my latest temporary job ending soon came to the front of my mind and it was difficult to get them out. I kept telling myself to be strong. It nearly worked.

The turning point came when I had just had enough of drinking fizzy drinks and I told myself I needed one more blow-out before I knuckled down to life on the sobriety highway, which in the end, I did.

I went back to my dad's caravan and I wasn't obliterated but I'd had quite a few to drink. I woke up in the morning and for some reason I just *knew* it was time to make a permanent change.

I had a disagreement with Dad and left his caravan and went back to stay in Derby - but 9th February, 2007, was the day that my life without alcohol began again.

May 2007 found me unemployed. The economic climate had changed and the days when I could waltz in and out of warehouse jobs were long gone. It was time to eat humble pie and make things up with my dad and move back into the caravan. It also gave me the opportunity to see my son.

Staying in my dad's caravan was never going to be a permanent solution. My dad and I had different opinions and although I did try to make the best of the situation, there was just no way I could stay there, so I left in early September 2007, with no job and nowhere to go.

Despite being homeless, I was determined that I would never drink or take illicit drugs ever again.

My days living on the street began under the arches in Loughborough. 'Seven arches' was what the locals called it. It's a railway bridge built with seven arches. One of them was over a river and on my first day of being on the streets it was where I decided to sleep.

I had no 'dole' money, no food, just a compulsion that I must get through that first night. I chose the arches because it was across the road from my dad's allotment, where his caravan was, and so I knew there was a water main on the grounds.

The water main would be a lifeline for me. I believed that I would physically suffer more from dying of dehydration than of starvation. This coming from someone who had wanted to drink himself to death for so long.

This was it. I was officially homeless.

I sat down under the arches and within a few minutes, it had sunk in. I had a few clothes in a suitcase with me. I had no means of shelter, so I quickly realised that it was going to be a very rough night. I started crying, inconsolably. How have I ended up here? I had cried many times before, but I knew these tears felt different. All the emotion came out. Strangely enough, getting it all out really helped.

It was still early afternoon and I had a lot of time on my hands. I was planning a lot in my head. Firstly, what am I surrounded by and how do I make it work for me?

As I looked around, I spotted what looked like a tarpaulin, the kind of material you'd pull over items you'd loaded on to a van.

I made my way towards it and realised that it wasn't a tarpaulin but the sleeping quarters of a disused tent. It was big and I wasted no time in bringing it back in the open to investigate it. The zip was working, it wasn't that wet inside and I realised that it was as good as I was going to get.

My mood brightened: at least I had shelter. I hadn't slept well the night before, so I just found a decent spot to put it down, got in, and to my amazement I fell asleep.

When I woke up it was still light, but I had no concept of time. It was a bit of a struggle to get out of my new living quarters.

From where I was, the nearest village was called Stanford on Soar. It is a very small, affluent village. After nipping over to get myself a drink at the water main on the allotment, I took a walk into Stanford. There was a church. My hope was that someone would be there and, hopefully, I could get some food. I was out of luck on that occasion. No-one was there.

There was pretty much nothing else in the village, so I decided to take a walk into Loughborough. I had no choice really. I needed to find some food, somehow.

When I got into the town centre, I didn't know what I was going to do. I didn't know the 'homeless' life. I just walked around a lot. I acknowledged a few people I knew and then I found myself in the library. I needed a rest and the library seemed like a good place to go. I managed to blend in and after a decent rest I made my way to the exit.

After leaving the library I turned right and saw a familiar face. It was Noah. I hadn't seen Noah in a bloody long time. He saw me and we acknowledged each other with a firm handshake.

Noah was a guy I used to talk to when I was out drinking in Loughborough; from the Three Nuns down to The Greyhound pub, we clicked. He had musical tastes that were like mine but, more than that, he was just a down-to-earth guy and I think we enjoyed each other's company. We would sink pint after pint talking about music until the cows came home. I have fond memories of our very drunken debates on top five e.g. top five Monday morning songs, pre-drinking songs, jukebox songs and so on. It was our homage to the fantastically, brilliant movie *High Fidelity* starring John Cusack and Jack Black.

He recognised that there was something not right and before he said anything, I told him I was homeless. He gasped. My body odour was beginning to become overpowering so he made the kind gesture of telling me I could go back with him and have a bath, something to eat and a change of clothes. I couldn't refuse.

Having a bath was so good. Good to feel fresh again. We spent a lot of time talking. I was beginning to fade quite quickly so I thanked him for everything and told him I had to get back before the night set in. He didn't ask me to stay, but I knew why he couldn't. I gave him a massive hug and I left. Having freshened up, the air outside was very nippy so I started to walk more briskly. It took a good half an hour to get back to the arches and I now had a sweat on. I got into my 'digs' and I settled in for the night. I woke up after what seemed like no more than an hour absolutely freezing. It was dark outside, and I was trying to work out why I was so cold. I didn't want to get out, so I just decided to grit my teeth and bear it and get through the next few hours.

The next day was pretty much the same. I went into the town centre, walked around a lot, sat in the park, tried to do 'something normal'.

Drinking never left my mindset and on many occasions, I had thoughts of stealing a bottle of Jack Daniels and going to join the other 'winos' in town. Plus, I could get so drunk that I would pass out in my 'digs' and wouldn't feel the cold. I didn't act on these thoughts. It wasn't me anymore.

I made my way out of the park and found myself at the library. I found a book to read and the only space available was next to a guy who was reading a paper. I noticed he was reading The Telegraph or The Independent. That's a posh paper to read, I thought. I was used to seeing people reading tabloid newspapers like The Star or The Mirror. What I noticed in the library was the amount of people that came in, sat down and used the facilities. It intrigued me to see how busy it was. People really did use a library!

The gentleman next to me fell asleep. I recognised a familiar smell. It was the smell of stale alcohol. I recognised it because I used to have it. It's the smell that no matter how much toothpaste you use, or how many extra strong mints you eat, it doesn't go away. The alcohol will seep through no matter what. The smell of his body odour and the stale alcohol was overpowering and after a closer inspection, I soon realised that he was probably in the same predicament as me, only he was still drinking. After a short time, he woke up, collected himself and his belongings and was on his way.

Being unemployed is hard.

Being homeless and unemployed is harder.

It was a very strange experience for me.

There were so many emotions that I went through. Some were momentary and raw; others were enormously incapacitating and stayed with me, even haunted me, for much longer than I ever thought they would. Living in unemployment prompted a lot of unknowns to run through my mind. I had no job and I had no money coming in. I questioned every choice I had made in my life leading up to this point.

I had a hard time taking stock of my life when I was possibly at my lowest point, because most of my thoughts inevitably focused on the negatives.

There were some bright spots in my life, both past and present. Being unemployed made me more resourceful and functional. Overall, though, I had to harden my mental strength to live through this. I found myself asking more questions about my life, and the answers were few and far between.

Despite all I was going through, I couldn't live without any money. So, I went to the Jobcentre to start an application for benefits. Back in 2007 it was Job Seekers Allowance that I had to claim.

I remember going to the job centre and asking how to make an application. The floor manager, Alec, who I spoke to that day was brilliant from the start. Everything was going well, and I managed to complete the application. I brought it back to Alec and he asked me one question: "The address section is blank, so could you tell me your address please?"

I told him that I was homeless and I didn't have an address. He replied that I couldn't claim any benefits without an address, although it could be a 'care of' address.

Shit. Where was I going to get a 'care of' address from?

I explained to Alec that I didn't have one and I didn't have anyone who could help me with this.

I asked Alec if I could use the Jobcentre as a 'care of' address and he said no. So, I took the claim form back off him and left the building. As I walked off, with no idea where I was going, a thought came to me. I decided to go to the charity The Bridge. They worked with the homeless and might know what I could do.

I walked in and I noticed a guy I knew from the soup kitchen at Project 5000. He was getting a bit out of line about his food parcel. He was acting like a spoilt child and being a bit of an arsehole because he'd got more tinned food than in his last food parcel. I couldn't help myself. I had to say something. I reminded him that it wasn't the fault of the female volunteer that he'd got more tinned items.

I told him there were people out there, like me, who appreciated the help offered and it would be someone like him who would spoil it for the rest of us.

I reminded him to choose his words carefully because his language was atrocious. He calmed down. Then I asked him to come outside for a quick chat and once we'd left the building, I asked him what was up.

He didn't respond straight away, but within a minute he was in tears and confessed to me that he had lost £400 on the roulette machine in the bookies!

I'm sorry to say that my first thought wasn't a caring one. My initial reaction was 'What the hell are you doing in there asking for a food parcel when you clearly have the money to spend on some shopping!'

Luckily, I didn't say that. For five minutes I just listened to what he had to say and then told him that I'd be happy to spend time with him once I'd got my dole claim sorted. I didn't go back to The Bridge. I went back to the Jobcentre. In my head I thought that I didn't want to be around other people who behave like this chap did. Their focus was different to mine and it gave me an insight that it was best to keep on my side of the road.

I made it back to the Jobcentre. I spoke to Elise on the floor reception (I noticed her name on her badge) and I asked if Alec was about. She asked my name and I obliged and gave her a short synopsis of how he had been helping me with my dole claim.

Alec arrived and I asked him again if I could use the Jobcentre for my 'care of' address, because I hadn't got one or any other avenues to help me. He must have heard the desperation in my voice because he finally said yes, I could. He said he hardly ever did this, and not to tell anyone.

What a relief! I thanked him and over the next couple of months, I was looked after so well by Alec and Elise.

When she was on duty, she'd spot me when I came in and would have my letters waiting for me when I came to the front desk. It was such a relief and a weight off my mind to have my dole money in place because it meant I could manage better, especially over the weekend.

Occasionally, I would treat myself to a nice, big, juicy fry-up in a café. Just being able to go to the supermarket to buy a green top pint of milk to use, instead of the UHT carton that came in a food parcel, to pour over my cornflakes, Weetabix or any other dried breakfast that also came with my food parcel, was a special treat!

After a while I moved my tent to a spot about a mile away from the town centre. I remembered from my football playing days that there was a massive playing field behind a local industrial estate where I could pitch it. I found a nice spot, on the opposite side from the business units, where there were some trees for a bit of cover.

Every night, before I settled down to sleep, I would urinate around the outside of my tent, in the hope that this would deter any foxes.

One Sunday night I had become a bit restless and couldn't sleep so I decided to go for a walk, and I came upon the industrial estate. I knew most of the businesses there as I had worked for a couple of the companies in the past. I had little to no money and I was trying to get through the next 48 hours until my 'dole' money came in, when I stumbled upon a depot for Ginsters, the well-known UK pasty and bakery company.

This was new to me. I saw someone walking out of the factory. I kept my distance, stayed out of sight and watched him emptying box after box into a skip. He was soon back in the factory and I ventured out with a little trepidation and hoisted myself into the skip. I couldn't believe my eyes. There was an abundance of pasties, sausage rolls and other savoury snacks just dumped. In a split second I realised I had to be in and out before someone came back so I shoved what I could into my pockets and went to jump back out of the skip, but it was too late. The same man re-appeared, and he frightened me as much as I frightened him!

"What the f---?! Who the hell are you and what are you doing?" he demanded.

I wanted to reply but I couldn't as I was still in shock. After taking a few deep breaths I managed to speak and told him I was sleeping rough and I'd seen all the food that was being thrown away. He didn't believe me at first because my clothes were quite clean, and I didn't look like a stereotypical homeless person. I explained to him that even though I was living on the streets, I didn't have to look like I was.

"You can come and see my tent, if you want. It's only over there," I said, pointing.

He declined and took me at my word. He didn't ask why I was on the streets and for that I felt relieved. We talked for a little while and he eventually said that if I came back on Sundays around 11pm, he would put enough savouries in a black bag to last me through the week. I was very grateful for this kindness.

As the dark nights drew in, I would light a fire every now and then and when my 'dole' money came in, I would buy a disposable BBQ and a cheap BBQ meat pack once a fortnight for a treat.

To-ing and fro-ing to the town centre became my routine. Instinct to survive had kicked in. Yes, I could go and find drugs and alcohol and drink and be high with all the other addicts and winos but in my head that would have been the easy option and an admission of failure.

My decision had been made and I had to survive in my way. This meant visiting the laundrette to wash and dry my clothes. At the local public toilets I spoke to one of the cleaning ladies. She said that I could have a shave there, as long as I washed the sink out afterwards. At the local leisure centre I talked to the manager who agreed that if I paid for a swim I could use the showers.

When my confidence was shaken, like the time I was verbally attacked by the father in the public toilets after speaking to his son, I found myself thinking back to my chaotic drinking and drug use. But this wasn't about me considering 'giving in' and going back to old habits. I knew I had to understand what was going on. I had to go back in my mind and understand more about what had happened to me and why.

One night in my tent, I was reading Al Pacino's autobiography. After I got to the point where I wanted to stop, I was in a very reflective mood. That night was one of the darkest since I had set up my home here and the wind was blowing steadily, as if God had turned on his air conditioning. I had secured my tent thoroughly and I lay there trying to think why my drinking and drug taking had taken me to rock bottom. I remember looking at the battery digital clock I had bought so I could still keep a sense of time and listen to the radio. The time was 20.03. I was spooked because if I took out the dot, it was the year that my son was born - 2003. Over the next four and half hours I began trying to untangle where my life had become poisoned by drugs and alcohol.

Over the weeks, I became a regular library visitor. The man I'd seen on my first visit, with the stale alcohol and body odour smell, was usually there reading his paper. One day I went up to him and introduced myself. He was a bit weary but he knew I was becoming a more regular visitor.

"My name is Enton, by the way," I said.

"My name is Atticus," came the reply, spoken in a very posh accent, something like a Major in the British Army.

Atticus was a very methodical man and always kept to the same routine. He always chose the same place to sit. He fell asleep at the same time, read the same newspaper and left the library at the same time, every visit.

I found it fascinating, watching this happen right in front of my eyes. I managed to get close to him and he allowed himself to talk to me and boy, oh boy, he sounded like an intelligent man.

On one occasion, a staff member at the library took a dislike to Atticus because he was fast asleep and snoring. She wanted him to leave. I had to step in and try and help him because I felt it was wrong. I just asked the staff member to put herself in his shoes. He was street homeless and all he had was what was in his camping bag.

"No-one in the library has complained about him and he just needs about another half an hour and then he'll be on his way. That's his routine," I said.

Thankfully, Miss 'I'm in charge here' listened to me. Right on cue, Atticus woke up half an hour later and off he went.

One day, he didn't appear. Sadly, news got back to me that he had succumbed to his alcoholism. It deflated me. I often wondered what his story was because he didn't really say much about his private life. We were never friends, but for a while I really missed his presence in the library.

The library became my 'homeless hub'; a place where I could keep warm in the day. Because I visited so often, some members of staff noticed and to keep them off my back I became a member. All I had to do now was pick a book and they would leave me alone. To mix things up, I would use a computer now and then or go into the quiet room where pretty much I would always get at least an hour's sleep.

After a kip, I would leave the library, just take a walk to stretch my legs, and try and act 'normal'. I would go into a few shops, look around, try to act the part of a regular customer who might be interested in buying a few items and come back to the library until closing time which on some nights was 8pm.

Being homeless, and living a hand-to-mouth existence, the advice I was given over time proved to be a godsend. I learned about the places where I could get some food and hot drinks during the week.

A voucher system was in place for people who were street homeless and because I was classed as this, I could exchange the voucher at a local church for a very adequate two-course meal (and seconds if needed) every Monday and Wednesday.

The staff at the church were so accommodating. Nothing was an effort for them. They listened to my circumstances without prejudice and never once talked about God. They knew why we were there, and it wasn't for the gospels.

Tuesday and Thursday were Carpenter's Arms days. They were a Christian rehabilitation centre. You had to queue up at the right time otherwise you would get stuck there for a while. It was hit or miss with The Carpenter's Arms. No matter how many times I told them that I had no access to any cooking appliances, they still put vegetables and microwaveable meals in my bag. A few times I managed to swap items with other people in the queue but not all the time.

Friday nights meant hot food at the Salvation Army. It is no longer operating there, but at the time the volunteers who gave up a few hours of their evening were awesome. They always made time to listen, feed us and at times, give us a sleeping bag or some clothes to take away with us.

The weekends were the hardest. There was no access to any food or food parcels during this time, so I had to save some of my dole money to keep me going.

CHAPTER 12

Homeless and not drinking – then a crisis strikes

Question: Can you be street homeless and not drink?

I think 99.9% of the time people would answer 'Are you insane?'

Of course you would drink on the streets, they assume, and who can blame them.

When a person is street homeless, they often use drink or drugs as a coping mechanism.

Luckily for me, I had already quit when I found myself street homeless, but that didn't stop me wanting to drink or take drugs.

I had daily thoughts. My brain tried to play games with me and run 'lovely' anecdotal memories of how good it would feel to be under the influence of my legal and illegal lovers.

The memories called to me, like an ex-girlfriend or boyfriend with the best seduction moves you've ever seen. It nearly worked, but an 'ex' is an 'ex' for a reason.

My conscience battled to keep me on the straight and narrow, but there was always that nagging voice trying to persuade me to give in - the 'devil on my shoulder', call it what you will.

Fuck right off, devil!

It would have been so easy to give in and become a permanent guest at 'hotel doorway' or in my case, 'hotel parkland' as a member of the street homeless tribe.

I would continue to ignore the siren calls to start using again, and luckily I had the willpower to do it.

How, I hear you ask?

Well, in my opinion it was simple; plain and simple. Surviving the street was my clear goal. I just had to survive. If I did that, I believed, then everything would fall into place.

I had already tried so hard to drink myself to death. My life had been reduced to unemployment, a tent, sleeping bag, ground blankets and soup kitchens. But I was now convinced I had to live and that meant not using.

One Wednesday night at the soup kitchen, a group of us were waiting for the van to arrive. I saw a man walking towards us. The best way to describe him would be that he looked like Father Christmas – if Father Christmas was living on the street without his red suit.

A few in the group clearly recognised him and they began to chat. Then, all of a sudden, 'Santa' - as I'll call him - announced that if we all put in £3 we could have ourselves a bit of a drink after our soup.

I told him straight away that drinking was one of the reasons why I was on the street, so I didn't drink any more.

He stared at me, with a look that said 'Who the fuck are you?' and then replied: "That's not my problem, son, so just put in your £3 and I'll drink your share."

Suffice to say that after my soup, I left them all to it. Sadly, a few weeks later, word reached me that 'Santa' had succumbed to his addiction and had been taken to the street in the sky. That was more motivation and determination for me. No way was I going to let the street take me to the 'street in the sky'. I looked the street in the eye and said, "Fuck you, street, give me your best shot."

Boy, oh boy, did it give me its best shot!

The sleepless nights were the worst. On many nights when it was hard to sleep, I would find myself walking around places just to be out and see street lights.

I had flashbacks. I vividly remembered coming out of Loughborough nightclubs, under the influence of ecstasy, cocaine and alcohol at 3am, without a care in the world. Here I was, walking past those same nightclubs, penniless and homeless.

As the days and nights rolled on, sticking to a routine kept me busy. It allowed me to foster habits that went with my goal of surviving and getting off the street.

My routine helped me to develop positive traits and eliminate triggers that would not serve me well.

Some days were good, and some days were bad. Very bad. I knew the very bad days would come; it was inevitable. But the good days could be very good. It was always a good day when the sun came out.

On a crisp, sunny, winter's day, I could at least get out of the library with a book in hand, head across the road to the park and read.

I used to watch people play in the park; families, young boys kicking a ball around or groups sitting on picnic blankets eating their food.

This was another way for me to keep motivated. For all the gratifying, instant rewards drugs and alcohol give, they don't give you reality. It's a false sense of security and a short-term solution. My reality was surviving for the long term, off the street and back into civilisation.

I opened my eyes.

As I tried to come round, I realised that I was in my tent. It was a Sunday. For a second there I was dreaming that I was asleep in my bed at my old flat in Loughborough. It was such a good dream.

In fact, I was fully clothed in a sleeping bag with two thick blankets over me, lying on four ground blankets and I still felt the cold.

I say 'fully clothed', what I mean is I was wearing a T-shirt under my hoodie, tracksuit bottoms - which were just about thick enough to keep me warm - and a pair of thick socks.

I didn't want to get out of my sleeping bag because I knew I was going to freeze my bollocks off, but it was something I had to do. You see, even on a Sunday, I still had to go and have a shower at the leisure centre and shave at the public toilets.

I counted to three...one, two, three... and I got out of my sleeping bag. I unzipped my tent and opened the doors to the world and you'll never guess what? It was flipping snowing! Snowing? No wonder I was bloody cold!

I ventured out to brush my teeth and it was so cold that I nipped back into my tent and grabbed my gloves. Within 15 minutes I had gathered together my toiletries and I was ready to leave.

I started to take down my tent (which I did every morning so no-one could see me) when I realised that I wouldn't have to because of the snowfall. It was coming down quite thick, so I decided to leave it up. It would be a decision that would cost me dearly.

The town centre was about a mile away, so it was nice to carry a lighter load for a change. The walk to town was bloody freezing. I made my way to the public toilets and had my shave and then it was on to the leisure centre for a welcome shower. It was lovely and warm, and I felt a lot better afterwards.

I took a stroll round town to see if any of the usual faces were about. They were nowhere to be seen.

The snow was starting to stick to the floor and a white carpet was forming at Market Square. With no money to buy a hot drink or food, I decided to head back to my tent. I still had Ginsters pasties and sausage rolls from my latest visit to the industrial unit.

The walk back was even more bitterly cold. When I got to where my tent should have been, I noticed a patch of ground that was clear of snow. I got closer and closer until I realised that my tent had gone.

My tent has gone!

My fucking tent has been nicked!

I couldn't believe it. Everything I owned in that tent had gone. I stood there with so much anger inside me. I shouted: "Who the fuck would do this?"

The tears began to fall freely. I looked up at the sky and shouted in anger. I completely lost it. Now I just had the clothes on my back.

I started to shake, mainly because of the cold but also due to rage.

I found myself walking. I don't know how, but I was walking. I ended up back on Derby Road and my rage was relentless. I began ranting and raving and shouting: "If I ever catch the person who nicked my tent, I'm going to fucking kill you!"

"Why has this happened to me?" I yelled.

The tears continued to flow. I couldn't stop them. I was completely devastated.

Looking back now, I wonder what it must have been like for the people driving past me when they saw someone completely losing their shit.

I managed to make it back to the town centre again and dropped down on a bench. I cried as I'd never cried before. I felt that I was completely fucked. No money, no food, no-one to help. Or so I thought.

Then a small lightbulb flickered on in my head. Maybe there was one person who could help me? Sonny was someone who knew my dad. I had met him because he volunteered at a Thursday night soup kitchen run by members of a local church.

As it was Sunday morning, I knew he'd be at that church. My spirits lifted a little as I started to make my way towards it.

I was in luck. The church service had not started yet, so I asked if anyone had seen Sonny and they pointed me in his direction. We shook hands.

"Come for the service, have you?" he asked.

"Not really," I replied. "I just wondered if I could have a quick word with you?"

Sonny took me to a meeting room at the back of the church. I told him that my tent and all that I owned had been stolen. I said I wondered if he had an old tent going spare?

Sonny said that he might have something back at his house, but I'd have to wait until the end of the service that was about to begin.

He told me to take a seat at the back of the congregation and we'd head up to his house afterwards. Brilliant. The relief was palpable.

As I sat and waited, I started to people-watch. I wondered what they must think of me and considered what I thought of them. They'd never seen me before and vice versa.

With the knowledge that I might get help, my anger subsided and I took in the moment. I was in a church watching people putting their hands in the air, singing loudly to what they believed was a man in the sky. They also listened to certain scriptures being read to them from a Bible.

As I continued to people-watch, some of the congregation glimpsed back at me. I eventually thawed out. It felt good to be warm.

Eventually, the sermon ended and I waited for Sonny to come and find me. A couple of people started talking to me and I was mindful not to be rude to them. I had no concept of time as there was no clock and I didn't have a watch. It felt as if I had been there for quite some time. There was still no sign of Sonny.

I started to think that I might have to go and find him. As I made my way to the front of the building, he saw me.

"So, are you still able to help out with a tent?" I asked.

"I am," Sonny replied.

I was so relieved that I felt I could start crying again.

I could have never, in a million years, expected what came out of Sonny's mouth next.

"Right," he said. "I have explained your situation to the church members and between us we have managed to raise £96 for you."

I was astonished. It was hard to grasp. The emotion was too much and the tears started falling again.

Sonny continued: "So now I am going to take you to buy a new tent and sleeping bag."

Unbelievable. My thought process was all over the place and I just kept saying in my head that these people didn't even know me, yet they were prepared to help me.

Why would they do this?

I know why now, but at that time it was something I couldn't get to grips with.

On the way to his car, I asked Sonny if he could thank everyone who donated their hard-earned money to me. I told him I was completely blown away by it all.

He said he would.

Ironically, the place where we ended up going to buy a tent and sleeping bag was literally less than half a mile away from where I had been camping.

Sonny asked where I was staying and I pointed out the spot to him.

With a new tent and sleeping bag at my feet, I told Sonny that he and his church members had made me feel something I hadn't felt in a long time - and that was humility.

Sonny replied: "No problem."

He went on to say: "Would you do me a favour? Would you come to a service at my church?"

In that moment, I felt obliged to say yes. How could I say no? We said our goodbyes and went our separate ways.

I made my way over to my patch and put up my new tent. Eventually, the night drew in and I settled down. My next train of thought was 'How am I going to get hold of some clothes or shoes?'

That night was a very testing one. My thoughts were all over the place but, finally sleep came.

CHAPTER 13

Meeting the Exaireo Trust – recovery begins

Carl Bard, the Scottish theologian, said: "No-one can go back and make a brand new start. Anyone can start from now and make a brand new ending."

I spent a big part of my life trying to put that quote into action. But I failed to 'start from now' on a regular basis. Most of the time I failed to take advantage of the opportunities that were in front me.

In winter 2007, with just the tent that the church members had bought for me and a few belongings, I encountered a homeless charity called The Exaireo Trust.

The Exaireo Trust provides rooms for the homeless in shared houses across Leicestershire. This was it. This was the moment I had to put things right and to start from now.

I'd first heard of The Exaireo Trust when I'd been to the local council and declared myself homeless. The council couldn't do anything because I was a single man with no-one who depended on me. The woman advisor told me that on Wednesday evenings, the manager of The Exaireo Trust provided some hot soup outside the library and it was worth speaking to her about being housed with them. She also gave me the number for the homeless advice centre called The Bridge. I turned up at their office and they asked me to come in and register and I received food parcels and vouchers in return.

On a melancholy Wednesday evening in December I decided to go and see the manager of The Exaireo Trust. Loughborough, I remember that the day was still trying to shake off its so-called winter and it was an intensely icy walk from my tent as the wind blew in from the west.

Destination, Granby Street. I arrived and there were some people hovering around near the wall outside the library. It wasn't long until a van pulled up on the other side of the road. A woman got out of the driver's side while a guy, who was wearing a high-visibility jacket, got out from the passenger side. This must be her, I thought. It was.

The chap with the high-vis jacket went to the back of the van and lifted out a box that contained a lot of thermos flasks.

They both walked over to where the group of people were mingling. I made my way there too. A warm soup was poured from the flasks into plastic cups and handed out with bread rolls.

I thought to myself, 'It's not the best-flavoured soup, but it's warm and it will do.'

I could hear a lot of moaning going on among the people in the group that had come early. Intrigued, I tried to listen (without being obvious) to what the fuss was about. I heard one say: "I thought you might have cakes and biscuits this week like you did last week."

The woman explained that they didn't have them every week, it just depended on who donated what.

I was just thinking, 'Be thankful you've got soup and some bread rolls because it's better than nothing.'

I saw the woman on her own and headed across to speak to her. I asked her if she was the manager of The Exaireo Trust.

She replied: "Yes. Are you here to volunteer?"

I laughed, not in a rude way though, and said: "Unfortunately not. I'm here to ask you how I go about getting housed with you as someone at the council told me you manage a homeless project."

She replied: "I'm ever so sorry. I didn't think you were homeless because of how clean you are. Yes, I do run a homeless project and we have an interview process so you would have to come for an interview first."

I said I had no problem with that. "The reason I don't look homeless is out of everything I've lost, I've not lost my dignity, so I look after my personal hygiene," I said.

She looked stunned. She then said that they were full, but she could take my number and get me in for an interview to get the ball rolling.

"I don't have a mobile phone, but I do have an email address that I can check at the library so could you email me the time, date and address when you need me to come for this interview?" I said.

She agreed and we said our goodbyes.

I made my way back to my tent and bedded down for the night.

I think the homeless charity manager's email came through about two weeks after that first meeting.

During those two weeks, I managed to catch up with Noah who, to my surprise, looked awful, dishevelled even.

He had the stereotypical 'homeless' look.

"Are you ok, mate?" I asked.

Obviously, he wasn't, but I needed to hear what he would say.

"Not really, Enton," came the answer.

He was very open with me and said he had split up with his girlfriend and now had his own flat but, since the break-up, most nights he pretty much drank himself to sleep so he could escape the heartache.

Blimey. What was I supposed to do?

I couldn't leave him to his own devices as he said he was going to the pub to start his day of drinking.

I asked him if he would do me a favour and follow me to a church where I was going to get something to eat. He agreed.

As we made the short walk towards the church, I explained to him that I couldn't stop him from drinking and that could only ever be his choice.

"If you want me to help you, in anyway, then I'm more than happy to help but I cannot come to the pub with you," I said. "You know my situation and why I'm on the street."

"Yes, of course. I understand," he replied.

We got to the church and I had a nice two-course meal with extras.

In fact, I demolished it. Man! I was hungry.

The church volunteers offered Noah some food, but he said no. I said my thank yous and off we went.

On the way out, I explained to Noah that I had a daily routine and it started with spending as much time in the library as I could.

"You are more than welcome to join me," I offered.

He said he was just going to have a drink at the pub and he may come back to see me on his way home.

I left it at that. I never thought in a million years that he would come back - but come back he did.

He was a bit drunk and said: "Why don't you come over and stay at mine?"

There were two things on my mind. One was that it would be nice not to have to sleep in my tent tonight, but the other was his drinking. It was obviously his crutch now and did I want to watch him drink himself into oblivion? If I left him on his own, was he going to be ok? I had to go with my gut instinct and I took him up on his offer. I couldn't leave him on his own. Maybe if he had someone to talk to, he wouldn't drink so much.

So, Noah took me to his flat to show me where it was and then I went off to take my tent down and bring it back to his house.

I arrived at Noah's flat and knocked on the door. He opened it and as I walked through, I took in the smell of stale beer – something I knew only too well.

His flat wasn't in the best state of cleanliness. It mirrored the disarray Noah was presenting, but I could manage it. I quickly saw the cans of lager Noah had bought. They were still in one of the flimsy blue and white striped bags the off-licence used. This was way before the plastic bag charge!

I was disappointed, but I understood.

Not long after I had arrived, there was a knock on the door. Noah asked me to go and see who it was. I opened the door and a man was standing there with a delivery of paint and decorating equipment.

He asked me if I was Noah. I turned and called: "Noah, there's a gentleman here to see you."

The man said there was no need to call Noah. He could just drop off these supplies from Charnwood Borough Council, and off he went.

I took the delivery through to the living room and put it in the corner.

Before long, Noah had consumed his cans and was lying on his settee. It didn't take him long to fall into a drunken sleep. He would appear to rouse himself, muttered slurred words, look confused and then fall back to sleep without really waking up. And, one last thing, was his massive SNORING!

With Noah asleep, I decided to make myself useful and began to clean up his flat. It took the best part of three hours and Noah slept right through it.

Once I had finished though, I felt it was all worth it because it looked like a flat again. When Noah finally woke up properly, he was completely shocked and very thankful for what I had done.

As the evening was ending, I decided to tell Noah about my weekly Ginsters run to the industrial unit. As I'd cleaned his kitchen, I'd noticed that he had the bare minimum in his cupboards, so I thought that the pasties, sausage rolls and slices would come in handy for him.

Later that night I took Noah with me to the Ginsters unit and the one time that I needed my contact to be there, he wasn't.

"Not to worry," I said to Noah. "Follow me."

I took him to the skip and opened it up. There was plenty for us to take home.

We arrived back at Noah's and had our feast. We watched a bit of TV before he took himself off to bed. He came back with some blankets for me and I bedded down on the settee for some well-deserved sleep.

The morning soon arrived and Noah seemed to be ok.

I put the kettle on and made us a cup of tea. While drinking our tea, I came up with a plan.

I said to Noah: "Look, I'll decorate the flat where it needs decorating if you let me stay here for the rest of the week."

"I'm down with that," he said.

The weather outside was dipping below freezing at night so I saw it as a great opportunity to be out of the cold weather for a few days and to help Noah through a difficult time.

I said to him: "I need you out of the way, so do what you need to do this morning and if you're drinking, please try to pace yourself."

Within two days I had finished decorating Noah's flat and it looked much better. I think Noah was pleased with what I'd done and glad of my company.

He said I could stay longer if I wanted, so I took him up on that offer but all that would change after another a week or so.

One night, when I was on my way back through the town centre from the Ginsters run, I bumped into Ian.

Ian and I had spent a lot of time together while I was living in my tent. I first got to know him when we met at Project 5000 soup kitchen at Emmanuel Church. I must admit I liked him from the start. I told him that he couldn't stay in my tent though because it was my home and I wasn't having it smell of rancid, stale sherry! He was a harmless, funny guy who would piss you off and make you laugh at the same time. He did like a drink though and when he did he was a fucking nightmare!

Ian wasn't street homeless and had his own flat, but for some reason he wouldn't stay in it unless he felt it was really necessary. When we met up in town, he would stick to me like glue. I told him from the offset that I wouldn't be engaging in any drinking.

As time went on, he would come with me to my usual places. He did try to behave himself, but as soon as he'd had a drink he would just play the joker and he knew it pissed me off. I soon got used to his antics though. The problem was other people wouldn't stand for it, so there were times when he ruffled the wrong person's feathers and it backfired on him. Ian came with me to Ginsters too, sometimes.

But the minute I introduced him to Noah that night it all went downhill fast, for both of them.

Ian asked if he could come back to Noah's and I said yes if Noah agreed.

We arrived back at Noah's and I introduced them. Noah was very welcoming and now briefly we were the three musketeers!

Their drinking started subtly. They would go out and about when I was having a shower, or when I was just chilling at Noah's. A few beers here and there. Then, they would start to bring cans back to the flat every three or four nights. Then, every two or three nights. I knew what they were doing, but at that time I was glad I was indoors instead of my tent because the winter weather was really kicking in. It was freezing out there.

Noah and Ian had more disposable money. We all put money into the pot for gas and electric as Noah's energy bills were on a pre-paid meter. Food was pretty much sorted with the Ginsters run and the soup kitchens so we never had to shop for much.

The final straw came when they literally collapsed through the front door with a pack of 24 cans of lager and a bottle of sherry, absolutely steaming drunk.

I was quite surprised that the drinks didn't smash and explode. I waited until they kind of composed themselves and said: "Please try to keep the noise and the drinking to a minimum as I'm going to get some sleep now."

Luckily, they were so drunk that I think they only managed a couple of drinks. I heard Noah crash about getting into his bed while Ian collapsed on the settee. Since Ian arrived at Noah's, I'd been sleeping on a camp bed, which was quite comfy.

The morning arrived. Noah came in looking terrible and Ian was just the same. I put the kettle on and made us all a hot drink. They didn't realise, but I had already packed my bag. Once they had finished their drinks I let rip. Not in a 'spitting feathers' way, but a controlled anger.

I said: "You pair are fucking, insensitive wankers. You know I'm trying hard to stay off the booze and here you two are blatantly throwing it in my face. I am not going back to that life because look where I'm at. You two can carry on without me."

I thanked Noah for letting me stay but added: "Now I'm out of here."

That was that. I didn't see them again for over six months and by that time I had managed to get a room with the Exaireo Trust. The offer of a room came early in 2008, a few days after I'd left Noah's.

I'd gone into the library early doors because I was bloody freezing. I just wanted some warmth. I logged into my emails and there it was - the offer of a room! I couldn't believe my eyes.

The relief mingled with tears. I was so overcome with emotion I struggled to breathe. I had forgotten that I was using a public computer and someone next to me kindly asked if I was ok and I replied happily: "I sure am now!"

The email said to go to their office on Park Road, Loughborough, for an interview at 2pm. I arrived early and knocked on the door. A lady answered and I asked if this was the Exaireo office and she said it was.

I explained why I was there and she let me through to the kitchen where she made me a cup of tea.

When it got to 2.20pm, I asked if the manager knew I was there.

She replied: "Yes, I've sent her a text to let her know you've arrived, but you'll soon get used to her being late."

Finally, the manager arrived, apologised profusely and the interview turned out to be a formality. Within an hour, and after a trip down to the council to submit my housing benefit claim, I finally had a roof over my head.

I was taken into the house, walked through the kitchen and there was my room. I even had my own toilet. I was now a resident of The Exaireo Trust.

Finally, after all those nights walking the street, visiting soup kitchens, doing the Ginsters run, spending hours in the library, I could put my tent away for good.

This was my opportunity to start from now and make a new beginning.

I was a resident for about a year. I loved everything about the project, especially the abstinence model it worked from. It was a balanced system of recovery. It gave me choices. Also, I was far away from anyone who could influence and entice me with the 'Just come for one drink or have one line'.

The charity had a work programme and I had to work for two days a week as part of my Licence Agreement. I loved it. I just loved being back at work and I didn't care that I wasn't getting paid.

I was working in a voluntary capacity with The Exaireo Trust's sister company G & S Services, a CIC (Community Interest Company). Most of the work involved house removals and garden clearances. Some of the houses and gardens were rancid. On one garden clearance we were pulling out old pushchairs from the undergrowth.

There was a house clearance that I vividly remember where I had to put on a dust suit and mask just to go in the house!

As time went on, and with the hours I was putting in, the managers of G & S Services paid to get my driving licence back, I had lost it a while ago due to alcohol related offences. They saw my potential and nurtured me to gain some supervisory experience. When it was convenient, I would supervise a group of residents myself. There was a bit of resistance at first, but when my fellow residents realised they had nothing to worry about, everything was cool. As time went on, I was working as a volunteer four days a week, and this never went unnoticed.

Living with other residents had some challenges, but that was to be expected because we are all different individuals. There was a cleaning rota for the house so we all knew what we had to do. If someone didn't pull their weight, it would be discussed. One or two of my housemates broke the rules and those issues were dealt with in the agreed manner.

My room was in a very nice house, ironically, not far from where my mum and dad were living. I used to see my dad when I was driving the work van and I deliberately ignored him as I wasn't ready for that reconciliation just yet. I was still living with my guilt.

The Exaireo manager managed to set in motion a way for me to see my son again and it didn't take long before he was staying over with me. There were many hoops I had to jump through for that to happen, and one was allowing Steph to see the place I was living in.

The months went by so quickly, but the thoughts of using drugs and alcohol were still there, more especially when the sun came out after a very hard, physical day at work.

I would have massive triggers where I could physically taste alcohol, whether it was a lager or a spirit. My nose would feel 'tingly' at the thought of snorting some coke and at the times when I felt worthless, taking some ecstasy would have gone down nicely. I couldn't take medication and be 'cured' of these triggers.

Recovery, especially in the beginning, was always going to be challenging. Each day was to have different emotions for me and there were times I thought about drinking and taking drugs daily.

I experienced 'pink cloud' syndrome, where I went through 'high on life' feelings during the first two months of my recovery, which are 'too good to be true' feelings. Although I never physically held drugs and alcohol in my hand, nearly every day I would think about a line of coke, ecstasy or a cold pint – but that's what they were, just thoughts.

Eventually, those feelings subsided. I was helped by the charity's Relapse Prevention programme, which is essentially about understanding, establishing and implementing strong coping skills and living an abstinence-based recovery. The hard work began when I learned how to deal with life's ups and downs without reaching for drink or drugs.

A Tesco supermarket was about a quarter of a mile away and it would have been easy to nip over and buy some beer, wine or spirits. Getting hold of illicit drugs would have been hard at first, as I didn't really know who was selling, but it wouldn't have taken me long to buy some.

I never succumbed to those thoughts. My drive in staying clean was as strong as ever. I knew there would be some tough times ahead, but I decided I was never going to fuck it up and end up back in my tent. I was now beginning to build relationships with most of the residents and I was able to draw alongside individuals who had come from an opiate addiction - heroin addicts to the outside world.

Watching how those people were surviving was a privilege. Most of them were on a methadone prescription and reducing. It was hard, at times, to see them go through their withdrawal symptoms. It gave me a better understanding of what a heroin addiction was like. I was that person who, in a previous life, shouted derogatory abuse at them while walking into the next pub ordering a pint and going to the toilet to snort a line of coke!

In 2009, all my hard work on the charity's work project paid off when they offered me a part-time job as a supervisor. I couldn't believe it! I did not hesitate before saying yes. From my first day on board with The Exaireo Trust, I knew that hard work would get me an opportunity to find a new job, but I didn't think for one second that it would be with the charity.

There was more good news to follow. Getting a part-time job was just the start of things coming together. Within a week I got wind of a work colleague who was looking to rent his old house out. I went to talk to him about it and it was indeed true. With help from another colleague in the Exaireo office, we did some calculations regarding my income and housing benefit. It worked out that it would be financially viable - just.

I was over the moon. It meant my son would have his own bedroom when he visited. My son and I lived there for about seven months until the cost of running the house became a struggle for me and I moved into a studio flat, which was more affordable.

In 2010, a staff member in the Exaireo office was moving on and leaving his role as a full-time support worker. One day I was coming back into the office after a hard day's graft when the charity's CEO pulled me into the office lounge and asked if I would like the job.

"Really?" I asked.

He didn't hesitate and told me the job was mine if I wanted it. I was gobsmacked. I'd believed that I could do it, but I didn't think a full-time opportunity would come so soon.

Back when I first had a room in the shared house with Exaireo, I decided to pay a visit to the Beacon Christian Centre. This was the church where the people had given me money to buy a new tent and sleeping bag. The church was about 200 yards around the corner from where I was staying.

I felt compelled to go because of what they had done for me and, to let them know that I was now off the street. I had built up a relationship with some of the congregation who ran their soup kitchen that I used to visit on Thursday nights. They'd always said to come and let them know when I managed to be rehoused.

As I walked into the centre, some of the members recognised me and gave me a hug and a warm welcome. Yep, they were huggers! They asked if I was stopping for the sermon and I said I might as well because it would be nice to catch up with everyone at the end.

Sermon over, coffees were made and conversations were in full swing. I was asked to come again and I genuinely meant it when I said I would - but, at that time, I wasn't ready. I went and stayed out of courtesy, not for the word of God.

Things would change, though. I found myself going to the centre more than I thought I would, if only for companionship. I didn't have real friends, so there was no-one I could talk to. My housemates were ok, and sometimes we would discuss our downward spiral into the abyss, but I didn't have anyone to talk to on my mental and emotional level that I felt truly safe and comfortable with.

The more I went, the more I formed relationships with people I would never have connected with in my previous life. I was invited with a few other residents to go to Snowdonia and walk the mountain. I jumped at the chance and it was an experience that will stay with me for the rest of my life. Why? Because when we stopped for lunch there was an unbelievable, amazing view that took my breath away. We were so high up that I could just spot a vehicle that looked like a three-inch micro machine toy car. I turned around to the rest of the group and said: "I can't believe that I have wasted so many weekends inside a pub getting absolutely obliterated when there is this natural beauty right in front of me!"

What an experience that was. My rambling and walking endorphins were released and I wanted to do this again and again.

The more I visited the church, the more the people from the congregation were nudging me to accept God into my life. I resisted.

I reminded them, politely, that accepting faith into my life meant having my own free will to make this choice.

The interesting thing about having faith in God is that it must be YOU that accepts him into your life. I think I'm a reasonable man who has been unreasonable at times.

I know that these people would be classed as 'happy clappers', absorbing Christian music into their soul and willingly asking God to move in their lives – but they were not that to me. These were intelligent people, who had come from many walks of life and were enthusiastic in their worship. I knew that I wouldn't be a 'happy clapper'. I just wanted to understand more about faith. I discovered that the church put on Alpha courses, which present the fundamentals of the Christian faith through a sequence of talks and debates.

It could be described by the church organisers as a chance to discover the meaning of life. I had completely lost my whole identity. Between the drugs and alcohol, I had become soulless. I was empty inside. I had no compassion, no empathy, no purpose. I booked on to an Alpha course and so began a journey of understanding the Christian faith.

I continued to go to The Beacon Christian Centre. It felt right to be there. After a few months, I left to go to another church. I felt like I needed to explore my faith further. This was a more reserved congregation, less 'happy clappy'. Months went by, then, before I knew it, a year had passed. I was beginning to feel stronger about myself.

As I moved into independent living, and with a full-time job now secured, visits to church diminished because my son played football on a Sunday morning.

Occasionally, I would drop into the soup kitchen at the Beacon Centre or a morning service at Kings Church when my son didn't have a football game.

I can honestly say, with my hand on my heart, that the people who I came across in my recovery have been wonderful. I would do an injustice to everyone if I singled out certain people. Many people have given me emotional and financial blessings over the years. I have tried to reciprocate when I have worked professionally, more recently, with others who were broken, destitute and lost.

Going to church wasn't just about discovering who God was. It was also about understanding a new way of life. This is best described in the park bench scene in the movie *Good Will Hunting* when Robin Williams' character Sean Maguire strips away the genius that is Matt Damon's 'Will Hunting' character layer by layer. He talks about art, women, love and war. It's one of my favourite scenes because of how honest and educated it is. The same could be said about having faith. A person must decide how they feel, who they are and who they want to become before allowing God into their lives.

Will you allow faith to capture the essence of God and follow him? Not many will, but for the few that do, I can only tip my hat to them. Me? My journey continues. I no longer go to church and I'm at peace with that. I'm at peace with most things in my life now because I now know who I am, how I feel and who I've become.

CHAPTER 14

Living in recovery

February 9, 2007: the date I chose to choose recovery.

The first week was the hardest, the first month was structured and the first year was a milestone I'll never forget.

In that first year, clean and sober, I remember working on a job for the local council and bumping into someone who was still street homeless. We had a quick catch up and I told him I had been clean for a year. Instead of saying 'Well done' or 'I'm pleased for you, mate', he said, without batting an eyelid: "Doesn't mean anything, mate, because you'll be back, and when you are, I'll have a can of Special Brew waiting."

If I ever needed any more motivation, then this was it.

In the 13 years since, I have never drunk alcohol or taken an illicit drug. I have seen that person on many more occasions over the years and I always make a point of reminding him of my years clean. Make no bones about it, recovery is hard work and it needs an appropriate attitude and a strong focus on learning skills to stay sober.

What was once a beautiful and destructive love affair with drugs and alcohol will now be a focused and critical journey in understanding that they will not be a part of me ever again.

Effective drug, or alcohol, recovery involves changing attitudes, obtaining knowledge and developing skills to meet the many challenges of abstinence. It also involves shifting my viewpoint on life, my behaviour and in some cases, my environment.

Being successful in recovery is encouraged by hope that recovery is possible and that I will recover. There's no going back.

Recovery had already started when I was homeless. No home, no job, no money. No nothing. Everything in my previous life was all or nothing. I had it all (to a certain degree) and then I had nothing. Just a suitcase and a tent. The question I ask myself to this day is, how the fuck did I stay clean and sober during this time?

Well, I believe it comes down to one thing - heart. What I mean is that you can be ruled by inner chatter in your head but once it's truly in your heart, anything can be accomplished.

Recovery was in my heart but in my head were the elements: every village and town had clubs, pubs and off-licences all offering me the medicinal support I had accepted and drunk for years. They also had the people who were offering some of the finest cocaine and ecstasy money could buy.

The inner chatter would lie, cheat and try to manipulate me to get what it wanted. It didn't care about me. It only cared about drugs and alcohol and it wanted me to feed the selfishness, which had fledged into something evil. I had become someone who only cared about cracking open that next can of lager or snorting a white line of Peruvian marching powder.

But it was in my heart where I was willing to be honest and open-minded and get what I needed; my recovery.

The cliché of 'one day at a time' was paramount during this time because each day was different on the street. Most of my time I was in survival mode and decisions I made were heart-led, such as showering, shaving, washing my clothes and so on. If I made those decisions with my head, there wouldn't be any need to visit the laundrette, shower or shave because I would have accepted the inner chatter telling me I don't need to do those things today, I could do them tomorrow. But, actually, tomorrow never comes.

I didn't recover from my addiction by just stopping 'using'. I recovered by making a new life for myself where, in the first instance, it was easier to use, but eventually, it was easier for me not to use.

If I didn't create a new life, then all the issues that brought me to my addiction would eventually catch up with me again and I wasn't about to let that happen.

I didn't have to change everything in my life. There were a few issues and behaviours that had been very troublesome, and if I allowed them to continue, I wouldn't have had a life to look forward to.

If I'd tried to hold on to my old life while in recovery, it would have led me to fail. I had been drinking and taking drugs for a long time. This had an effect on my brain that had been used to certain daily and evening alcohol routines and drug experiences. I suffered from overwhelming cravings when I would see, smell or taste something. The cravings were a reflex to external or internal triggers, and this would have a massive effect on me as I tried to abstain from drugs and alcohol.

The sun is a great example of this. When it shone down from a bright, blue sky, I would reminisce about being in beer gardens and at BBQs, remembering vividly the ice-cold beers and all-day drinking experiences.

I gained knowledge and understood the nature of cravings and triggers during my twelve months as a resident with The Exaireo Trust. I was able to use the tools I learned in their Relapse Prevention programme and others that I found. Over time, I grew confident in my ability to minimise them. But, it was far from easy. There were massive triggers and cravings, some that could stay with me for hours.

Sometimes, all I could do was think about drinking, which in turn made me think about using cocaine and ecstasy. Getting to three months clean and sober was a great milestone. Admitting my faults, owning them and learning to grow from them was now the key.

The success of my recovery was never down to me alone. I had help. Once I received that help, it was about keeping moving forward. No two days are the same in recovery, because cravings or triggers can pop up over mundane things. I found early in my recovery that I had a lot of time on my hands and no idea what to do with it. It was then that I discovered the gym. I went down to the local leisure centre with another resident and we did a workout consisting of free weights. I loved it. It just made me feel so good and it certainly filled some of my time.

At first, I worked out three times a week. Then, I incorporated some cardio exercising, specifically running. I think it was in 2012 that I completed the Loughborough Half Marathon and The Winter WOLF run.

It wasn't long before I was training five days a week and it made me feel fitter in mind, body and soul. It took a long time to heal my body and shift my mental framework but now I can't think of a better way to start the day than going to the gym and smashing my body for an hour!

I have been weight training for nearly eight years now and I still love it to this day. It is still part of my recovery and will be until the day I leave this earth.

Together with gym training and running, I worked more days with the charity's work programme. While I was working with other housemates and residents of the charity, I developed a keen interest in studying substance misuse because I wanted to help people get their lives back on track and understand why this had happened to me. There must be more to it than me just saying that I loved drinking and taking drugs?

To start my journey on this new career path, I paid for an online drugs and alcohol counselling course, which I quickly completed. Then, I found out about a foundation degree course in Drug and Alcohol Counselling that was being offered at the University of Leicester for four years, part-time. The main condition for this course was that a person had to be six months clean and sober.

This means that there would be two things to celebrate when I reached the six months milestone: 1) I was six months clean and sober 2) A four-year degree course was waiting in the wings.

Man, I was super excited.

A couple of months into my degree, I made the brave decision to contact my parents. I literally lived about a minute's walk away from them. I went to their house and knocked on the front door. My mum answered. She wasn't expecting to see my face. I said I just wanted to let her know that I was ok and I had a room in a shared house and I'd started university.

As time went on, my relationship with my parents began to grow again.

Over the four years of my course there were highs and lows and I wanted to quit on more than one occasion. I had many late nights studying but moreover, I met some good people. Some of them were in recovery, but others weren't. They were from all walks of life and a select few were already working in the treatment or recovery field.

One of the tutors had such an impact on me with his knowledge that I was always waiting to pick his brains. He also introduced me to Mindfulness and at first, I was the biggest sceptic. Over time, and with some softening around my hard edges, I embraced it.

In 2013, I graduated. My parents and grandparents were there to see me receive my degree. It was a moment when we could all be proud, not least because I was the first person from our family to successfully go to university.

During my years in recovery, I'd been so busy working hard in my supervisor role with the charity's work programme, and studying, that it was hard to believe that time could go by so quickly.

I do remember having some powerful cravings during this period. There were times when I thought about drink daily, but I was never so powerless that I acted on them.

In 2010, I had started to see someone. I had begun working for Youth Shelter, a homeless charity for 16-25-year olds. Part of the role involved sleeping-in.

I don't remember how I found out, but there was a woman called Layla who fancied me. I must admit, I fancied her as well. We started off well. There was an instant attraction between us and we managed to spend one Christmas together before it came to an end after about three months. I suppose some of my insecurities played a part in us going our separate ways as I didn't really cope with her not wanting to see me as much and so I gave her a piece of my mind about it and the rest is history. I sometimes wonder how that could have played out, but it was never meant to be.

Life carried on and now everything I had worked hard for was beginning to pay off. I started to play football again. A colleague at work put me in contact with a Christian team called Loughborough Emmanuel and I managed to play about half a season with them until I called it a day. A mixture of old age and losing a bit of passion for the game made the decision for me.

In the summer, I played cricket for Loughborough Outwoods for about three seasons. In my final season, I ended up captain of the Second team. Cricket would take all day. My son would come with me when it was our weekend together and it was nice for him to be around, playing with other kids.

I would eventually go on to play rugby with Syston Rugby Club, after 20-odd years out of the game. What a club to play for! I have been welcomed in like I am one of their own and there are some top boys within the Third and Devs teams. My first game was against Harbury and it was to be a bus trip to remember.

To be playing sport again was everything to me. It's in my DNA. Telling my new teammates about my addiction was easier than I thought it was going to be. I think there were some who couldn't believe it.

It was hard at times when most of the team had their wives and girlfriends come down to watch our matches, but I never let it get to me.

I had prepared myself for the single life after my last liaison, but then I met someone again. Her name is Vicky Bailey and she has two daughters, Katie and Sophie.

Vicky had been a volunteer psychotherapist with The Exaireo Trust and she never lets me forget that the first time I met her I was quite rude. Apparently, I ignored her when I was in the office studying. I probably did ignore her although in my defence, I have a vague memory that she didn't hear me say 'hello' and acknowledge her.

It was probably about a year later, when the charity had grown and moved into a much bigger office, that I next saw her. She was now a frequent fixture in her psychotherapy role. She would come into the office I shared with other colleagues and say 'hello' to everyone and this time I did much better and we had whole conversations together.

I do have a confession to make though. When Vicky came in to meet and greet us, and then go about her day, I would always take a sneaky look at her bum as she left. It was, and still is, a gorgeous bum.

As time went on, Vicky had a set day when she worked at the charity. Sometimes, we would get to speak together and sometimes it was just a 'hi and bye' as I went to do my job in the community.

One day, I was office-bound and I came down to answer the front door of our office. The enquiry only took a couple of minutes and as I turned round I saw Vicky come in for her scheduled day and dissolve into tears.

I quickly ushered her into our lounge and asked her to wait there. I came out to see the residents she was supposed to see that day and told them that due to unforeseen circumstances, Vicky wouldn't be able to see them that day.

I went upstairs to my manager's office and told her what was happening and then went back to see how Vicky was doing. I just said that I would sit in the room with her.

When Vicky managed to compose herself, she told me that over the past year she had been working hard to save her marriage, but to no avail. A divorce was imminent.

I don't know how long we were in the lounge before Vicky got up, thanked me and left to go about her day.

Four months passed, and although Vicky continued to work with the charity's residents, we would only see each other in passing.

She did tell me that her divorce had been finalised. I said I was sorry to hear that. Vicky thanked me again for what I'd done and I said anyone would have done the same thing.

As the months went by, I finally plucked up the courage to ask her out for lunch. She accepted. Food was ordered and as we were eating, I just came out and said to her: "Well, you know about me, so what do I need to know about you?"

She laughed. I think it broke the ice. We talked for over an hour. There were quite a few things to talk about, especially our expectations. Thoughts of 'Is this a rebound?' sprung to my mind.

I listened to how Vicky talked about her marriage. I told her I was sad to hear her marriage had ended and I had genuinely hoped it could have been saved.

I told her: "I never expected to be here with you now, so I'm intrigued to see where we go from here."

It was something for Vicky and me to ponder and as the weeks turned into months and we spent more time together, I started to recognise that something could happen between us.

There was a bigger picture regarding our respective children to think about. We agreed to see each other, minus the children, to start with and then I would come over on my own for tea one evening for a gentle meet and greet.

I gave Vicky the time to be with her girls while they were adapting to life without their dad and vice versa with my son.

I was living in a lovely cottage which my son and I had made a home. I would sometimes have my nephew over to stay, mostly on the weekends when my son stayed over.

As time went on, Vicky and I grew very close to one another and we were spending a lot of time together at each other's homes. The inevitable milestone came, and my son and I met Vicky's girls. It was inevitable that they would be apprehensive about building a relationship with me, so I prepared myself for all possible reactions. I think the introductions went as well as could be expected.

Over the next few months, I would stay at Vicky's place with my son and, on occasions, my nephew. All four of the youngsters worked out how to play together and I remember one time when Katie and Sophie had persuaded the boys to play hide and seek at Vicky's house. There were echoes of laughter coming from all around the house.

Eventually, the topic of moving in together was put on the table between Vicky and I. Her marital home had been sold and guess which village she moved to? Yep, the one where I was living.

It was nice to have Vicky closer and be able to walk to her house and vice versa. We just spent a lot of time together when there were no children. My son and I would stay over one night with Vicky and the girls on her weekend. This was our routine and before long, the time came to talk about the inevitable. Moving in together. I was very resistant and I did put up a fight for as long as I could. As much as I put up a defence, I knew that Vicky was right, so we did it.

Holy shit! It hasn't all been plain sailing. I would have worried if it had been. I'm very set in my ways, while Vicky is a very independent woman. We clashed. Many times. You know what we did once the emotion was reduced? We talked. Like adults. I didn't do that before. If I was angry or my need wasn't met, I would act all child-like, chuck all my toys out of the pram, pack my bags and go and get wasted, suffer the consequences and not recognise the harm it caused. I couldn't do this with Vicky. Not just because I loved her. Not at all. No matter how fraught the issues may be, everything comes down to making the right choices that are best for both of us and not just a selfish need of mine. Just like every day for the past 13 years, and every day for the rest of my life, I will make the right choice not to drink or use drugs.

It has been an eye opener living with Vicky. Vicky loves to be around the right people, whereas I'm happy in my own company. I think it does piss her off that I don't seem to want to leave the comfort of my own skin. I have learned though, that I can have both!

Vicky and I have friends and, together with her family, we all get together and invite each other round to our respective houses and have dinner. We call this Dinner Club. Sometimes I end up being like Scrooge, huffing and puffing about all the negatives! She tells me I'm a 'bah humbug', which is very true. I would rather be at home watching one of my favourite films of all time, *An American Werewolf in London.*

Anyhow, back to Dinner Club. These three-course meals are a bit like the TV show *Come Dine with Me*, without the scoring, the voiceover and a lot more enjoyable. There is an abundance of food, drink, laughter and genuine companionship. What really makes it special for me is watching how Vicky and our friends drink and *enjoy* alcohol. I started off consuming alcohol in this way but eventually, I would end up drinking to oblivion. Vicky and our friends drink a lot but not in a way that would meet the indicative measures for alcoholism. Far from it. They drink in this way because it is part of having a good time and they don't continue to drink the next day or the day after that. It is the same with birthdays, weddings and Christmas. It really does fascinate me how Vicky and our friends are able to do this, and it is somewhat cathartic watching them drink alcohol responsibly.

I suppose that is drinking in a nutshell, really; people coming together as social animals and enjoying the pastime of drinking. I have been in pub, clubs and at parties and drunk myself 'sober'. In the beginning of my recovery, it felt weird not to be drinking. Why weird, you ask? Well, alcohol was like a friend, offering all its wonderful medicinal support for many years but now I drink soft drinks and non-alcoholic lagers without a care in the world.

Before recovery, I would have gone into an insecurity tailspin anxiously waiting for the first couple of pints to take away the butterflies before I then went onto the main course of a filet mignon of beers, spirits and cocaine.

Now, I have learned to understand and cope with my insecurities and I am at peace that I will never drink again. I have turned out to be the man I wanted to be. I was a man who always used to be seduced by the murmurs of the alcohol demons, but now I'm strong enough to resist their devilish charms and just be me.

I no longer take cocaine and consume alcohol. I am substance-free. I am enlightened. Like the parting of grey clouds. I have accomplished my goal. Living a drug and alcohol-free life gives me the capability to distinguish the world entirely unblemished by hallucinatory, psychedelic and addictive drugs.

The understanding of self-determination drives my mornings. I rise, undamaged by the visions that drugs and alcohol characteristically piggy-backed into my life. This brings an incomparable happiness. I have transformed the innermost me. I have a wry smile when I see men and women come out of a boozer, unable to walk because they are completely drunk. I can't help instantly thinking something hypocritical, forgetting for a moment that that used to be me. I used to start drinking moderately and accelerate to drinking completely out of my mind.

Of course, I can have my bad moments where my mood swings into frustration and anger and I become a challenge to be around. According to Vicky, Katie and Sophie, I am a 'grumpy pot poo pants' and I have the T-shirt to prove it. I snore, I break wind and I know I can be a nightmare to live with at times, but Vicky still wants me around and sleeping in the same bed together.

I found a new respect for reading when living in my tent and Vicky and I love watching boxsets on TV. There are sides of my character that have changed beyond the bounds of appreciation. During the days of my drinking and drug taking, I repeatedly flew off the handle with rage and caused significant destruction both physical and emotional. I was completely self-centred, and I sought out immediate satisfaction taking everything, everyone, and myself for granted. I unquestionably joined the irresponsible group of people who didn't give a fuck. I couldn't understand that I had fashioned a necessity for my self-indulgent behaviour because it was a false existence.

My world didn't become immediately better once I stopped drinking. A radical change came from within. Life now is more tranquil, unassuming, and varies from one day to the next. I have found love again which, at times, I feel I don't deserve.

Vicky and I have been together for some time now and we will grow old together. She has an understanding of all the devastation I have caused and never holds it against me. I held it against me for so long and I didn't want to forgive myself. I persuaded myself that the alcohol and drug-taking part of me was who I really was.

By replacing the drugs and alcohol, I have permitted myself a look at who I really am.

EPILOGUE

So, we reach the end of my story – for now.

I am an addict.

I live in recovery and that is what I choose every day.

Every hour, every day, every week, every month I make a choice to not drink or take drugs – now for 13 years and counting.

Every day is a new day in recovery. Every day I choose to remain abstinent and I choose not to drink or take drugs, which enables me to manage many emotions such as anxieties or vulnerabilities.

Most days I can feel like that little boy, the younger me, vulnerable, scared, anxious or angry and I know that fragility. It would be easier to disappear, get off my face and never return.

My life today has improved beyond measure. I sometimes find myself, metaphorically, pinching myself as I can't believe I have Vicky and her two girls and together we are building a life.

We work hard to be happy and contented with what lies ahead for us. We go out for meals. I can accept that alcohol is social and enjoyable to other people and they can have fun without being off their heads!

I have now, as Vicky puts it, softened my hard edges. I still experience anxieties and anger. At times, I get so angry that I am beyond using words to express how I feel. I have hit the depths of naked vulnerability when I want to drink, party and experience those feelings of euphoria from the years when I used drugs and alcohol to mask my emotions. Every day is a challenge to manage my state of mind, especially now I am clean and sober.

Before I chose recovery, when my emotions were heightened or triggered, I would flick on the 'fuck it' switch and leave, disappear and get completely wasted. Now, if I did leave, or fall off, the sobriety train, I know there would be no coming back. Why? It's simple. Guilt. I would experience the massive ferocity of guilty feelings. I would take my tent and rock up in an area where no one would know me and drink until I was unconscious. The problem is, when I do hit the big emotional responses I always want to run and get off my head.

The battles I have with these impulses are exhausting. The mental strain from any trigger leaves me wrung out, but surprisingly stronger for the decision I make to remain clean.

I have a new addiction: going to the gym and working out. It supports my choice and it is my haven, my arena, my safe space. Here, I can lose myself with my music and get the endorphin-hit to support my recovery. I have fallen in love with sport again and I have trained and qualified as a rugby coach. I work with the Leicester Tigers as a sessional coach in their community team. I also have a voluntary role as BUCS 3 & 4's Team Manager/Co-Coach at Loughborough University and support Loughborough Grammar School team as a coach.

I am studying for a BA (Hons) degree in Sports Management. If someone had said to me a few years ago that I would be following my sports passion and taking a degree, I think the response would have been very colourful and blue!

The perfectionist in me is challenged every day by this new and exciting path. The vulnerability of looking foolish, or not knowing what I'm doing, plays within my head. Am I worthy to be in this arena?

Sometimes, the inner chatter is louder than others. Some days are a bigger battle than others but I move forward by focusing on my love of sport and growing in the confidence and the belief that I can do this!

I've always been honest with myself.

I loved drinking and taking drugs. I loved how they made me feel. I also know I can never drink or take drugs again... not a single drop, pill or line again.

So, I dig deep within myself, day in day out. I've learned what addiction means.

FROM THE FAMILY ALBUM

I've chosen a few of my favourite photos from the family album to share with you on the following pages. They are all special moments in my life and bring back loads of memories.

I spent many enjoyable hours playing football and cricket on this patch of grass near my home

Just a short walk down here to the mainroad where I hitchhiked

My childhood home in Johnston, Pembrokeshire

With my niece in Shelthorpe, 2006

Zach and me in Shelthorpe, 2003

Drug and Alcohol Counselling Graduation Ceremony with Mum and Dad, 2013

Rugby - first season back and two trophies! Players' Player of the Season and Most Improved Player, 2017

Chillin' in Norfolk with Vicky and the campervan, 2017

Vicky and me, 2017
Life is good!

ACKNOWLEDGEMENTS

There have been so many people who I have come across in my lifetime that I probably could write a chapter on just their names!

Unfortunately, I can't do that here. There are, however, some people, which include some inspiring women, who without their support, I would never have finished this book.

Firstly, to my girlfriend Vicky Bailey, who has loved, supported and championed me emotionally, psychologically and financially with this book. She has pushed me so far out of my comfort zone from the day I decided to make this book a reality. I well and truly now know what 'networking' is because of her! I love you Vicky Bailey.

Next, my Editorial Consultant Elaine Pritchard of Caittom Publishing, (signposted to me by Vicky!) who listened to my story and then tirelessly made my words more enchanting for you all to read. Regular meetings and endless emails were arranged and sent between us for her to give out shrewd and encouraging feedback, held me accountable and applauded me every step of the way! I couldn't have done this without you, Elaine.

There's my genial publisher Sarah Houldcroft at Goldcrest Books. From our first meeting onwards she became another person who passionately placed faith in me and the book.

To Rachel Hargrave, at RDZ PR Ltd, who is a more recent addition to the book team -I look forward to the PR/media blaze trail!!

Thank you to Hannah Dickens of Hannah Amy Photography for working with the world's most reluctant model (me) for the book's cover picture.

To my Mum (Cody) and Dad (Eric), who have always been there - even when I may have been a complete nightmare. I finally understand what unconditional love means because you continue to show me this. To my son Zach, my nephew Brandon, my brothers Jason and Justin and to my Grandparents Eric and Iris, who are just two special people I get to call Nan and Grandad. To *all* my family in Johnston, Milford Haven, Merlin's Bridge and Haverfordwest, Pembrokeshire. Here are some who need a special mention: Uncle Guff, (who likes to give everyone a nickname!) and Aunty June (who always used to say "Mind the road now, love, and don't talk to no strangers" when I was younger!), Bogroll, Terence, Tracey Esther, Uncle Shinky and Aunty Minnie, Skunky (Wayne Sheehan), Kay Sheehan, Carl Sheehan, Tracey, Sharon, Jo and Sturley. To the family members I have lost along the way, especially my Uncle Vivian, Uncle Albert, Aunty Celie and Uncle Robert. To Karl Boswell who has settled in the Rhondda Valleys. The list would be endless as I have a lot of family dotted around Pembrokeshire and beyond, so, to you all, I give you a shout out!

To Stevie James, a top goalkeeper, who put me through my paces early on in my goalkeeping journey. He taught me almost everything I know!

To Shehzad Malik, who is like a Jedi when it comes to addiction and recovery. I've lost count of how many times I sought your help with my assignments on my degree course and you always had time to give the right guidance. We used to have fantastic discussions on music too!

To Rob & Karen Glover of www.thebuzzco.com who always gave me a place to stay and for expanding my Motown/ Northern Soul musical tastes into a journey of Psychedelic Funk, Acid Jazz and Hammond Grove masterpieces. I'm sorry I soured our relationship and I hope you guys are well.

To Chris, a legend in your own right and former teammate for the now disbanded Sileby WMC football team, and a friend who has lived through most of my best memories.

CONTACT ENTON

www.therealbarefoot.co.uk

Instagram: entonbarefoot

Facebook: Enton Barefoot

Twitter: @EntonBarefoot

Printed in Great Britain
by Amazon